Recipes from
Our Front Porch

HEMLOCK INN

BRYSON CITY, NORTH CAROLINA

THIRD EDITION

Recipes from Our Front Porch

HEMLOCK INN
BRYSON CITY, NORTH CAROLINA

3RD EDITION 2012

Printed in Canada

ISBN-13: 978-0-9647083-9-6

Cover design by Scott McGrew
Text design by Stephen Sullivan
Interior and cover photographs by Morris White
Photographs on pages 5, 10, 43, 53, 101, and 113 by Ricke Hester
Edited by Amber Kaye Henderson and Susan Roberts
Produced by Keen Custom Media

Cover: Our guests return year after year. Here on our front porch, they meet
new friends and renew old acquaintances through the years.
At our early-morning coffee, served on the patio, not only is the day
started in a majestic setting, but also our guests share knowledge of
our world out there, share recipes, and talk about our food served
here—thus the title of our cookbook, *Recipes from Our Front Porch*.

This book is dedicated to my precious mother, Ella Jo Shell, who left us all too soon in 1998. She left behind a legacy of good times, character, grace, and this amazing collection of recipes. Thank you, Mom, for everything. I love you dearly and miss you.

And to my father, John Lewis Shell, who has patiently allowed us to work in the family business for 25 years now. I am certain that there were times when he wanted to pack our bags and move us out, but he did not. Thank you, Daddy, for this privilege. I love you!

ella jo

I had an amazing mother. She was the mother everyone wished they had. She was smart, funny, organized, spunky, and generous—essentially the life of every party. When she walked into a room, usually talking, you knew she was there.

She could throw together an amazing meal in 15 minutes. When I realized she was dying, I honestly stood and watched her in the kitchen, thinking, "Surely I can do this." I still can't.

Born Ella Joe Stevens in 1930 (she later dropped the "e" in Joe because she thought it was too masculine) in Kingsport, Tennessee, Mom was a proud graduate of Dobbins-Bennett High School and Tennessee Wesleyan College, where she met my father. They were married at the young age of 20 just before Daddy was drafted into the army. Most of their married life was spent in Marietta, Georgia.

When my parents bought the inn in 1969, Mom was in her element. She truly had the gift of hospitality, and the Hemlock Inn was her playing field. Her smile greeted you through those saloon doors with a comment that made you feel as though you were the only one in the world. She had more "best friends" than anyone I knew. Everyone thought she was his or her best friend. Lucky me—I knew she was mine.

john's blessings

My father, John Shell, did not just bless the food before breakfast and dinner at Hemlock Inn. He also blessed people with his jovial personality and stories about almost everything. His simple presence in a room blessed people. One thing Mort and I realized soon after we moved to the inn is that we could not replace my parents. We could only attempt to do their job with the same intentionality and zeal as they did. My father's prayers are special, and if you have been fortunate enough to hear him pray, you know that he often weeps. God shows up when Papa prays.

You will find Daddy's prayers scattered throughout the cookbook. Read them and let them bless you as they have many others before you. I might add that on the rare occasion when I am asked to pray before the meals, I simply read his prayers. Inevitably, someone will make a point to tell me, "You pray just like your dad." I guess they really do have their eyes closed!

Our dear Heavenly Father, how glad we are to start this day with Thee, and we pray that somehow Thou would help us to see that it is not what comes our way that counts, but rather what we do with what comes our way. We thank Thee for Thy strength and mercy and now for this food. In Jesus' name we ask it. Amen.

contents

preface

Old Apple Tree

There's a bend in the road on Galbraith Creek where an old apple tree grows very near the curve. I remember the first time I saw it. A calmness came over me that I hadn't experienced before. It was early spring with snow on the surrounding mountain peaks, but tiny buds were already visible on the old tree. Since then, 13 springs have come and gone, and every time I get to that bend in the road, I still find peace and serenity—whether spring, summer, fall, or winter!

That's the feeling at Hemlock Inn. It's a special place! It would be impossible to write a cookbook without telling a little about the place where all this good food is cooked and served so bountifully.
—Ella Jo Shell, 1982

My mother wrote that 30 years ago. The apple tree is long gone, but the feeling is not. As you weave up Galbraith Creek on your way to Hemlock Inn, there is indeed a calmness that comes over you.

While a lot has changed in 30 years, we take great pride in the fact that so much at Hemlock Inn is still the same. Our food is prepared by local ladies who love to cook, and our menus are much the same as Mrs. Haynie's from the early 1950s. (Mrs. Haynie was the original owner of Hemlock Inn.) Though most of the recipes we use are Mrs. Haynie's, many of our family recipes have also been added. All of the food we serve at Hemlock Inn (with the exception of our Apple Chips and Pumpkin Chips, which are available for purchase at the inn) is in this cookbook. Our goal is to provide you with a little Hemlock Inn to take home.

So, as Mom said, let us tell you "a little about the place where all this good food is cooked and served so bountifully."
—Lainey Shell White, 2012

introduction

Most people who write a cookbook are known for their cooking and/or spend a good amount of their time cooking in the kitchen. I, on the other hand, am neither known for my cooking nor do I spend much time cooking in the kitchen. I was 12 years old when my parents bought the inn, and as I grew up, I watched people cook and served what people cooked, but I cooked very little until I got married.

The joke is that my husband, Mort, and I moved to the inn so he could have fried chicken twice a week. In reality, it is less of a joke than we originally thought! Mort loves fried chicken, and I cannot fry chicken, so the arrangement works pretty well. However, we did raise three boys, and the inn does close for a few months each year, so I am called upon to cook every so often. Sister Jeanne's Chicken (on page 99) is a family favorite; served with wild rice and steamed broccoli, it makes a great meal.

My mother wrote the original cookbook, and I have simply been given the honor of revising and updating what she spent so many years compiling.

So come along with me while I take you on a journey: the story of Hemlock Inn and of my mother, as told through these incredible recipes.

Hemlock Inn is much more of a feeling than a place. Yes, it is a rustic 60-year-old mountain lodge sitting on a scenic hilltop (elevation 2,300 feet) nestled quietly among the majestic pines and beautiful dogwoods of the western North Carolina Appalachian Mountains and just a short drive from the Great Smoky Mountains National Park. And yes, our guests are drawn to the inn because of its genuine Southern hospitality, its accessibility to many outdoor-adventure day trips, and its natural peace and tranquility that resonate from its 57 wooded acres. Yet, if you were to ask many of our guests why they choose to come back to Hemlock Inn year after year, their responses would consistently include one major reason. While they come for all the other reasons, they also come for the food.

Hemlock Inn serves two large, plentiful, family-style meals each day. Perhaps it can best be described as Southern-style, made-from-scratch comfort food. It has always reminded me of eating at my grandmother's house. That is probably because, rather than chefs, our inn hires local ladies accustomed to cooking and seasoning food for their own families. The chicken is pan-fried just like my grandmothers would make it, in a black skillet over a gas range. The green beans are seasoned with fatback, the corn on the cob and tomatoes come from local gardens (like my Granddaddy Stevens had), and the desserts and rolls are homemade. The food is bountiful, with an assortment of vegetables and fruits along with the main dishes. Served family-style around large lazy Susan tables, the meals present an overflowing amount of food and choice for everyone.

Each mealtime is preceded with a blessing and ends with wonderful conversation and laughter as guests share stories and adventures of their day and about their families. Lasting friendships have been born and regularly renewed around the tables over the past 60 years.

In the spring and fall, you are greeted each morning by a warm fire and a hot cup of coffee. Even in the summer, the morning air is cool and crisp and the coffee is most enjoyed on our porch overlooking our beautiful mountain view.

Hemlock Inn is for everyone who wants a quiet change of pace, change of scenery, engaging conversation, and, oh yes—a great, home-cooked Southern meal!

history

Hemlock Inn was built by Seth and Lorene Haynie in 1952. In fact, an old road sign that reads HEMLOCK MOTOR INN was recently uncovered in the basement. The sign is appropriate considering that most of our rooms are easily reachable from a car.

In the 1940s, the Haynies bought 65 acres of mountain property on Galbraith Creek Road in Bryson City, North Carolina, from Plumer Plemmons. The property is located just 1.5 miles from Great Smoky Mountains National Park. At the time, Mrs. Haynie had been retained to feed the construction crew that was building the Tennessee Valley Authority's Fontana Dam. She had previously been in charge of food service at Emory University in Atlanta, and Mr. Haynie had been a real-estate agent in Decatur, Georgia. Upon retirement, they built the inn, situated on top of a small mountain at an elevation of 2,300 feet.

The original building had only nine rooms, one of which was where the Haynies lived. In 1958 a second building with 12 more guest rooms was added, and in 1965 the Red Cottage was built. The Rondette was added in 1968, the Woody Cottage in 1971, and finally the Innkeepers' Cottage in 1990. The inn now has 20 individual rooms plus four cottages.

In the early years, the inn operated without a telephone and was open only during the summer. Spring and fall were soon added and became very popular times. Now the inn stays open through December, mostly to accommodate families riding the Polar Express Excursion Train. We also open in the winter months for groups and special occasions.

The Haynies sold the inn to Georgia and Raymond Johnson in 1964, and the Johnsons sold it to my parents, John and Ella Jo Shell, in 1969. All of the innkeepers have resided on the property.

This is where I come in . . .

I was 12 years old when my parents bought Hemlock Inn, and my sister, Dianne, was 15. Our home at the time was Marietta, Georgia, where my father was born and raised and where he was in the insurance business. It was quite a change for two city girls to come to the mountains, but we loved it. It didn't take long for us to settle into the simpler, quieter lifestyle.

I use the word *lifestyle* because that is what it is. There are days when I wonder if anything else is really going on in the world. Things move a little more slowly here, and we like that.

I was asked many times growing up if I would ever come back to the inn, and my answer was always, "It depends on whom I marry." Well, I guess I married the right guy. I married Morris "Mort" White in 1983 and moved back to the inn in 1987 with our first child, Andrew, who was 20 months old. Steven was born the next July, and then came John Thomas in 1991. After 25 years, our adventure continues.

memories of hemlock inn

My first memory of Hemlock Inn is as a 10-year-old, sitting at one of the lazy Susan tables eating corn on the cob with a family from Iowa. My dad was an insurance agent, and the current owner of the inn was one of his clients. Our family had accompanied my dad on a routine business call. Two years later, my dad came home and asked what we thought about buying the inn. I thought he had flipped. I cried myself to sleep, not able to wrap myself around the idea of leaving all my friends and the only life I had ever known. My parents bribed my sister and me with horses, a dream we had always had. Later I discovered, much to my dismay, that horses were not my thing.

Six months later, in the spring of 1969, my mom and I were packing up our Marietta, Georgia, home with my best friend, Sue, and moving to Hemlock Inn. My dad had already moved to the inn, and my sister had conveniently signed up for every conceivable summer camp known to man that summer. She was unavailable to help pack and unpack.

The original idea was to drop me and Sue off at a Girl Scout camp in the backcountry of Pisgah National Forest near Brevard, North Carolina. After fording a few creeks in a torrential rainstorm on an extremely muddy dirt road, our little 1964 Volkswagen Beetle slid off the road into a tree, which saved my life but also took two of my front teeth and busted my face pretty badly. With that, camp was ditched and we called my dad, who was about an hour and a half away in Bryson City, to come get us. That's the bad news; the good news was that Sue and I had moved to the mountains together. She stayed with us until August, when her mother insisted she come home and start school.

That summer was a fantasy. We sat on the front porch, talked to the guests (especially the cute guys), ate the best spaghetti ever, and fell in love with Hemlock Inn.

mealtime

The highlight of the day at Hemlock Inn is easily mealtime. Breakfast is served at 8:30 a.m. every morning, and dinner is served at 6:30 p.m. every evening except Sunday. A genuine dinner bell, usually rung by a young guest, announces that the meal is ready. Five large lazy Susan tables, each seating 10–13 guests, have been bountifully set. Guests file into the dining room and find their way to the tables. The guests remain standing while a short blessing is offered, a tradition, started by Seth Haynie, that dates back to the very beginning of the inn.

As guests sit down, the unique nature of a Hemlock meal begins. Some around the table may be friends or family members. Others may not know anyone with whom they will be sharing the meal. But that soon changes. Small, polite conversation begins. They will share the events of their day and where they are from, but more often than not, they discover a common bond. Conversations become more animated and genuine. Stories are told and laughter fills the room. The conversations last through the meal, dessert, coffee, and often much longer. Friendships, some that will last for years, are formed.

We often wonder what we would learn if our tables could talk. We have witnessed two men discover that they worked together in South America for PanAm, one as a pilot, one an air traffic controller. They had spoken for years but never met until they were seated together at Hemlock Inn. We have seen a son, grieving the recent loss of his father, encouraged after finding a grief counselor sitting with him. Countless times, guests discover a neighbor they never met or a colleague. We constantly find intriguing people with fascinating stories or lives. Everyone has a story. Our tables provide a means for these stories to be told.

Psychologists often report how important mealtime is for a family. It is the time a family catches up with each other. The same thing happens to the Hemlock family. It is a special time.

lazy Susan tables

The lazy Susan tables are a special feature of Hemlock Inn. The original antique table, which dates back to the 1850s, still sits in the middle of the dining room. Close examination reveals that it was constructed with pegs. It was in the possession of the Haynie family and stored in a barn in Georgia. When the inn was built, they decided at the last minute to bring it with them, never dreaming it would be popular. Assuming guests would want to have private dining, they also brought a number of drop-leaf tables from the chemistry lab at Emory University. Much to their surprise, everyone wanted to sit at the large table. Eventually, the lab tables were abandoned, and Jack Grant, a wonderful craftsman from Maggie Valley, was hired to build four more lazy Susans.

Now the tables represent the very essence of Hemlock Inn more than any other single feature. Guests have called and asked for their measurements, and some have had duplicates made. When speaking to a prospective guest on the phone, it is not unusual to be asked, "Is this the place with the lazy Susans?" Perhaps the tables' greatest feature is that they allow guests to sit, eat family-style, and have conversations easily without ever having to interrupt a story to say, "Pass the peas, please."

menus

The menus have varied very little over the years. The few times I attempted a change, it backfired . . . either with the cooks or the guests. For instance, there are reasons we have casseroles. First of all, they are delicious, *and* they fit in the oven when our stovetop is full. There is a balance I discovered. You can't have too many items on top of the stove or in the oven either. Our guests also have come to expect certain dishes on certain nights. One thing we learned: Don't take away country ham on Wednesday and Saturday nights!

Everyone has a favorite. Here are some sample menus:

BREAKFAST	DINNER	HOLIDAY
Scrambled Eggs	Fried Chicken	Turkey/Dressing/Gravy
Sausage	Rice/Gravy	Baked Ham
Cheese Grits	Meat Loaf	Green Beans
Fresh Strawberries	Green Peas	Sweet Potato Casserole
Yogurt	Apricot Casserole	Apple Cranberry Casserole
Granola	Carrot Custard	Creamed Corn
Biscuits	Broccoli Salad	Mashed Potatoes
Bran Muffins	Apple Chips	EJ's Cranberries
Orange Juice	Pumpkin Chips	Apple Chips
Coffee/Hot Tea	Yeast Rolls	Pumpkin Chips
	Chocolate Cake	Yeast Rolls
		Pecan Pie/Pumpkin Pie

our cooks

The question has often been asked of both Mort and me, "Are you the cook?" Our answer is always the same: "We *can* cook, we *will* cook, and we *have* cooked, but if we *are* cooking, something terrible has gone wrong."

Contrary to the popular trend these days, we purposely do not hire chefs. We prefer to hire local ladies who know how to cook and properly season genuine Southern-style food. The chicken is fried in an iron skillet on top of a gas range, not deep-fat fried; our biscuits and desserts are made from scratch; and yes, our green beans are seasoned with fatback. Everything is real, not frozen, prepared food. It is grandmother cooking—we think the best kind.

The inn has two shifts for the cooks. The morning cook comes in around 6 a.m., prepares breakfast, and then helps in the early preparation for dinner, such as making casseroles and desserts. She will leave around 11 a.m.–noon. The evening cook comes in around 2 p.m. and finishes dinner.

We have been very fortunate to have wonderful cooks over the years. Annie Sitton and Myrtle Mask were the cooks when we moved here in 1969; Mrs. Sitton retired two years later. In those early days, the inn was only open May–October (we're now open April–December and some winter weekends), and there was no such thing as unemployment insurance to get the cooks through the winter months. Myrtle's goal was to work as many hours as she could while the inn was open. She would work the morning shift, take a short break, and come back and work the evening shift as well. She took one day off every other week.

Sadly, Myrtle, our dear friend and cook, died opening day of 1978. She called my dad early that morning to say that she did not feel well and to ask if he would please take her to the hospital, where she died shortly thereafter. We were devastated. Our neighbor, who happened to be superintendent of schools at the time, asked Mom if there was anything he could do. She said, "Not unless you can make biscuits." He said, "I *can* make biscuits," and he did every morning for the next two weeks! One morning, he asked if he could take some to work because his secretary did not believe him. Since then, Mort and I have learned to keep some fresh biscuits frozen because we don't make biscuits either!

Since Mrs. Mask died in the late 1970s, we have had numerous cooks come and go, all with the gift of cooking. Our line is, "If you can read and measure, you can cook at the Hemlock Inn." Actually, there is much more to it than that. Our cooks pour out genuine love and pride in everything they create, and we are so very grateful to have had each and every one of them. Our special thanks to all of those who have kept our tradition of wonderful home-cooked meals alive and well at Hemlock Inn.

our guests

My dad has always said, "Hemlock Inn is not only a place; it's also a feeling." He's right, and it's because of all the wonderful guests who come year after year. From what I have been told, Mr. Haynie, the original owner, personally checked out all the prospective guests before he would rent them a room. Hemlock Inn operated for two years without a telephone, so folks just saw the sign on the side of the road and drove up.

While Mrs. Haynie was cooking, he carefully scrutinized every one of them. He would walk to the parking lot, chat a little, and either invite them in or not. They had to pass his test. Mrs. Haynie, anxious for guests to try her dinner, would question him. He would either say, "They are just not our kind of folks," or "They will be really happy here. I put them in room 6." Mr. Haynie knew early on that Hemlock Inn was not for everyone. Thus began the history of Hemlock Inn folks.

When the Internet became the way to communicate, Mort would say, "I still want to talk with them." One guest questioned him by saying that some folks may not want to talk on the phone. Mort's reply was quick: "Then I'm not sure how happy they will be sitting around a lazy Susan table eating breakfast and dinner with total strangers."

But guests at the inn are not strangers very long. As innkeepers, we often like to take credit for that. The truth is that the old-timers and repeat guests are the ones who do that for us.

We take a risk if we try to single out specific guests, but we must mention a few. Doris and A. R. Tyson of Atlanta knew the original owners and were instrumental in getting my parents to purchase the inn. They were regular visitors to the inn for well over 50 years, leading hikes and helping out with anything that needed to be done. Louise and Gerald Abbott also came for more than 50 years. In fact, they came so often that some of their friends were convinced that they were part owners. Louise never denied it. Frank and Rose Smythe only came once a year . . . for six weeks. They famously announced that each generation of innkeepers was allowed only one change. W. H. and Velda Woody loved the inn and the Smokies so much that they spent the entire season with us for 14 years. They personally built the Woody Cottage for their use, later leaving it to the inn. The list goes on and on. They are among many, many others we simply refer to as Hemlock Inn folks. We love each of them.

our boys

Oh, my! The subject of raising children at Hemlock Inn could take up an entire book, one that you would find in the comedy section. When we decided to come to the inn in 1987 to work with my parents, our oldest, Andrew, was 20 months old. I found out the day we moved in that I was expecting son number two, Steven. John Thomas came along in 1991. During the height of country inns in the 1980s and 1990s, it was well known that children and innkeeping did not mix. I guess we proved that wrong—or not, depending on how you look at it!

Since one of the reasons we moved to the inn was to relieve Mom and Daddy, we decided to move into their house, which was physically attached to the inn and contained the inn telephone line, night doorbell, and all the alarms. The Innkeepers' Cottage was built in 1990 for my parents . . . our lives changed forever. Not too many years later, when our third son, John Thomas, was rather young, he raced into the home yelling, "I didn't know our house was stuck to the inn!"

So Mort and I raised our three boys at the inn. They were perhaps the pickiest eaters on earth, but somehow they managed to find something to eat each night, and as the years went on, they gradually ate more and more and discovered their favorites. Their favorite night turned out to be Wednesday. However, one recent summer, John Thomas was home from college and announced that Tuesday was not his favorite night (though it is Mort's), and he was going to Bojangle's. He said, "All I ever eat on Tuesday is chicken and rolls." When I asked what he was getting at Bojangle's (knowing the answer), he sheepishly said, "A chicken biscuit." He then decided to save a few dollars and stay home for dinner!

My children have done and said some funny things over the years. Riding their tricycles through the dining room during dinner, asking a guest sitting next to them how old she was, and offering all the kids on the patio free candy and drinks (though at least insisting, "My dad has already paid for everything") are the first that come to mind. They also called the cooks "the cookers" and the waiters "the bringers." After his first day of kindergarten, Andrew sat down at the dinner table, hung his head, and cried, "I can't be nice anymore." It had been a long day!

John Thomas used to talk about his friends, my friends, and Mimi's friends. That was what determined their age. When he was 5, I once had to get him out of one of our guests' rooms (we were already in bed and realized he was not in the house). The parents were asleep while he was coloring with his friend!

Steven was our costume guy. The only issue was that he didn't want anyone to see him dressed up. That was a problem with guests being everywhere!

But the most fun was Wiffle ball in the front yard. Once, while the inn was closed, we let them use a hard ball, only for the ball to bust our van's front headlight because we had forgotten to move the van.

If school was out, there was always a ball game in the front yard and often a guest would volunteer to referee when the competition got tense. A home run was a ball in the parking lot.

Those were great days.

All three boys have been known to move the lazy Susan table during the blessing (while everyone else had their eyes closed) to make sure that the fried chicken was in front of them.

The boys have each worked in all areas of the business, mostly in the dining room. But all three have spent their season in the office, have hauled garbage, made runs to the laundry and grocery store, painted, cleaned gutters, and raked leaves. You can't live at an inn and not be engrossed in the 24/7 nature of the business. I have often thought how proud my mom, their Mimi, would be of them.

They all have turned into amazing young men, and we miss them when they are not around. However, they are the first ones we call when we need a postcard put together, a fresh idea, or something edited (for instance, this cookbook). Most recently, Steven and his bride to be, Sarah, announced that they would like to get married here in our front yard.

Thank you Andrew, Steven, and John Thomas for making innkeeping fun! We love you dearly!

Hemlock Inn is all about family—ours and our guests'—past, present, and future.

Our Boys' Favorite Menu

Beef Pie	Baked Apples
Country Ham with Red-Eye Gravy	Green Beans
Creamed Corn	Hemlock Inn Yeast Rolls
Wilted Lettuce	Honey Bun Cake
Banana Fritters	Hemlock Inn Sweet Tea

Note: Our boys' favorite recipes are indicated throughout this cookbook with a

mountain adventures

While many folks come to our mountains to participate in the abundant outdoor activities of the area, some come to visit other wonderful attractions.

The Cherokee Indian Reservation is just a few miles away and features the Oconaluftee Indian Village and Museum of the Cherokee Indian, as well as a number of shops that exhibit and sell authentic Cherokee baskets and carvings. The Great Smoky Mountain Railroad in Bryson City offers daily four-hour excursions into the mountains, as well as the immensely popular Polar Express during the Christmas holiday season. Fontana Dam, the largest dam east of the Rockies, is also nearby. For those wishing to go a few more miles, George Vanderbilt's beautiful mansion, the Biltmore House and Gardens, is located in Asheville, just one hour away. Surrounding towns and communities offer wonderful shopping, crafts, and eateries and are well worth a day's adventure.

nature at its best

The beauty of the Smoky Mountains is undeniable. One of the great fortunes of Hemlock Inn is that it is located just over a mile from the most-visited national park in the country. The Great Smoky Mountains National Park is 814 square miles of forestland and contains more than 850 miles of hiking trails. The trails can take you along rocky mountain streams and waterfalls or up to mountaintops with indescribable views. You can take a pleasurable short stroll or hike for as many miles as you wish. The Appalachian Trail traverses the entire length of the park along the crest of the mountains. The park is also an International Biosphere Reserve with more than 10,000 species, conservatively, of plants and wildlife. It is quite simply a nature lover's paradise.

This paradise extends well beyond the park boundaries as well, with outdoor activities that resulted in this area being named one of the best outdoor areas in the country. There is world-class white-water rafting in the Nantahala Gorge and all sorts of boating activities on Lake Fontana, a 17-mile man-made lake that is part of the Tennessee Valley Authority. The mountain streams provide some of the best fly-fishing anywhere (they are also great for tubing!). Mountain biking, zip lining, rock climbing opportunities, and so much more abound!

Hemlock Inn guests don't really have to go very far from the inn to enjoy nature. Our rustic mountain lodge is surrounded by nature. Situated on a small mountaintop and located on 57 wooded acres, the inn has incredible mountain views, a mile of hiking trails, and a closeness to nature rarely found in today's upscale, sterile environment.

All four seasons are experienced over our months of operation. Guests experience the fullness of new green growth and flowers in the cool spring, the warmth and deep greens of summer, the brilliance of color in the fall, and the cold, clear skies of winter. In a single day, visitors may experience a cool morning, followed by the heat of midday, and a wonderful afternoon mountain rain before returning to the coolness every evening brings. The average summertime high is 83°F, cooling to 58°F in the evening.

While at Hemlock Inn, you may witness deer in the meadow below the large deck just off the dining room; hummingbirds fighting over the feeder in the front yard; bluebirds nesting in one of several boxes located on the grounds; cicadas, katydids, and crickets singing in the early evening; and perhaps even a pesky raccoon, looking for food at night. Nature's creatures fill the forest surrounding the inn. There is nothing more fun than watching children catch fireflies in the evening after dinner.

You may also get the opportunity to meet bumblebees, spiders, or even an occasional black bear or rat snake. They are all part of the wonders of nature at its best, all part of God's marvelous plan and design.

deep creek

If you turn left out of the Hemlock Inn drive and go just a mile and a half, you enter the Great Smoky Mountains National Park and discover Deep Creek, nature's paradise. Deep Creek is one of the numerous streams that flow out of the park. It is fast-moving and filled with smooth rocks, creating a wonderful white-water adventure. Too shallow for rafting, it is the premier tubing site of the Smokies. It is also highlighted by three waterfalls that capture your imagination and miles of winding hiking trails that follow every turn of the creek. You can take a short stroll, admiring the mountain laurels, rhododendrons, or flame azaleas in season, or take an extended hike on its loop trail (which was an old logging road where I actually learned to drive in the 1970s). Unmatched fly-fishing is available beyond the tubing area, and there are even horse trails for the equestrian. It is such a special place that our oldest son, Andrew, went there to propose to his now wife, Jeanette. She refers to Deep Creek as his backyard.

We often say that a trip to Deep Creek should be required by all our guests. The road from the inn is a quiet side road not traveled by many. We refer to it as our private entrance into the park. Once there, you will forget whatever ails you as you enjoy the fresh, cool water, listen to it cascade as you walk the trails and view the waterfalls, or challenge the trout in its currents. It is an adventure you will want to experience over and over.

basic information

While Hemlock Inn takes great pride in tradition, it is important to let you know of a few changes that have taken place over the years. For instance, we no longer cook in peanut oil. Instead we use vegetable oil, though you certainly can experiment with that.

In the original printing of *Recipes from Our Front Porch*, a few corn bread recipes called for ½ cup of bacon grease. We now use vegetable oil. (Though John Thomas went to college with a new griddle and "accidentally" forgot to clean it after frying bacon for breakfast. He said the grilled cheese sandwiches for lunch were delicious.) So again, experiment! (Try half bacon grease and half vegetable oil!)

On occasion you will see lard in the original printing, but we now use shortening. Accent is no longer used at any time. In our dressing recipe, we have changed chicken fat to vegetable oil.

Our sausage is still made fresh and purchased at a local meat market.

We still make our own breadcrumbs from unused rolls and biscuits, and we make our own bacon bits and salad dressing.

We cook with gas at Hemlock Inn. Remember that all ovens are different, and because your altitude may be different from ours (2,300 feet), you will need to adjust your oven and length of baking time according to your situation. All good cooks fool around with recipes and come up with good results. Feel free to do this with ours.

Our kitchen is busy in September and October with the production of apple and pumpkin chips. We have continued (at Mrs. Haynie's request) the tradition to keep their recipes a secret. However, you will find them available for sale in our gift shop and for consuming at dinnertime. There is nothing better than apple or pumpkin chips on a hot, buttered, homemade Hemlock Inn yeast roll!

BEVERAGES

Our dear Heavenly Father, we are blessed because we know Thee, and we come now to give Thee thanks. We are so glad Thou dost love us and call us by our first name, and our prayer is that we would do what is pleasing to Thee. We thank Thee for this lovely day and for Thy love and for watching over our families. We thank Thee for this food now. In Jesus' name we ask it. Amen.

Hemlock Inn Sweet Tea

4 family-size black tea bags
1½–2 cups sugar

Pour a kettle (8 cups) of boiling water over 4 family-size tea bags in a teapot and let steep 5–10 minutes. Remove teabags. In a separate small pot, bring a small amount (about 1 cup) water to boil. Remove from heat, add sugar, and stir until it is completely dissolved. Pour tea and sugar mixture into a 1-gallon pitcher. Fill the pitcher to the top with cold water. Stir and serve over ice.

Yield: 1 gallon

Tim's Russian Tea

2 cups sugar
1 tablespoon ground cinnamon
2 teaspoons ground cloves
4 individual black tea bags
1¾ cups unsweetened pineapple juice
1¾ cups unsweetened orange juice without pulp
1½ cups orange juice without pulp
¾ cup lemon juice

Boil 16 cups water, sugar, cinnamon, and cloves together for 5 minutes. Meanwhile, let 4 tea bags steep in 2 cups boiling water for 5 minutes. Combine the two mixtures and add juices. Let mixture simmer for about 30 minutes. Serve hot.

Yield: 1½ gallons

Lib's Almond Punch

6 cups pineapple juice
4 cups ginger ale
1 tablespoon almond extract
½ cup sugar

Mix all ingredients together. If desired, add more sugar and flavoring.

Yield: 12 servings

We are often asked about our sweet tea. Our secret is twofold: We only use decaffeinated Luzianne tea for iced tea (Lipton is best for hot tea), and we make a sugar mixture to make the tea just right.

Alcohol

Recently, while sitting on a beach, I struck up a conversation with a group of ladies, and they asked for a Hemlock Inn brochure. One of them immediately eyed the photo of the lazy Susan table laden with fried chicken. Another gasped, "Oh, my, they don't serve alcohol." The other quickly said, "Oh, I just can't picture any kind of alcohol around that table." Maybe that's why we have never served alcohol. For whatever reason, the tradition continues. Our inn is alcohol-free.

Annie's Instant Spiced Tea

1 (18-ounce) container powdered
   orange drink mix
¾ cup instant black tea
1 (3-ounce) package powdered
   lemonade mix
1½–2 cups sugar
1 teaspoon ground cloves
1 teaspoon ground cinnamon

Mix all ingredients well. (If desired, the amount of spices can be increased.) Use 2 well-rounded teaspoons to 1 cup boiling water for each serving of tea.
Yield: Approximately 4 cups powdered mix; 64 servings

Nancy's Tea Punch

6 individual black tea bags
½ cup sugar
1 (8-ounce) can frozen lemonade
1 cup water
1½ cups pineapple juice
1 cup ginger ale or lemon-lime
   carbonated drink

Brew tea for 2 hours in 4 cups boiling water. It's very strong! Mix in other ingredients.
Yield: 12 (6-ounce) servings

Millie's Hot Milled Cider

16 cups apple cider
16 cups cranberry juice
12 whole cloves
2 cinnamon sticks
pinch of allspice
1 cup sugar

Combine all ingredients in saucepan and heat over high until sugar is dissolved, about 10 minutes. Cool and reheat. Remove cinnamon sticks.

Yield: 25 servings

Note: This recipe is best if prepared the day before it is served.

Sally's Cranberry Tea

10 cups water
4⅛ cups container cran-strawberry juice
¼ cup lemon juice
2 cups sugar
4 (3-inch) cinnamon sticks
1 tablespoon whole cloves
3 family-size black tea bags
1 cup orange juice without pulp

Bring first 6 ingredients to boil in large Dutch oven. Reduce heat and simmer 10 minutes. Remove from heat and add tea bags. Cover and steep 5 minutes. Add orange juice. May be served warm or cold.

Yield: 16 (6-ounce) servings

Sally Jenkins was one of my mother's many friends.

Hot Chocolate Mix

1 (25.6-ounce) box powdered whole milk
¾ cup powdered coffee creamer
1 (21.8-ounce) powdered chocolate
  drink mix
1 (16-ounce) box confectioners' sugar

Mix all ingredients together well. Store in an airtight container. Use 3 heaping teaspoons in 1 cup boiling water.

Yield: Approximately 1 gallon powdered mix; 80 (8-ounce) servings prepared

Note: We use Nestle Nesquik for the powdered chocolate drink mix.

Agnes's Mocha Punch

¼ cup instant coffee
3 cups sugar
16 cups (1 gallon) milk
2 cups chocolate syrup
6 cups vanilla ice cream
6 cups chocolate ice cream

Mix instant coffee, 4 cups water, and sugar together in a saucepan and bring to boil (do not boil). Then turn down to simmer and let simmer for 5 minutes. Refrigerate for 2 hours. Combine milk and syrup in separate bowl. Add ice cream. Stir well. Just before serving, pour coffee mixture in punch bowl. Add milk and ice cream mixture to punch bowl. Stir and serve.

Yield: 25 (8-ounce) servings

EGGS & CHEESE

Our Heavenly Father, we are so thankful that Thou dost continue to watch over us and care for us. We pause now to sing Thy praise. We lift our hands and hearts to Thee for this good day and Thy mercy. We thank You for Thy love. We thank You for this food and the hands that prepared it. In Jesus' name we ask it. Amen.

40

Grits Soufflé
1½ cups quick grits
4 cups grated Cheddar cheese
12 tablespoons margarine
3 teaspoons seasoned salt
1½ teaspoons hot sauce
3 eggs

Cook grits according to package directions, omitting salt. Add cheese, margarine, salt, and hot sauce to grits. Beat eggs well and add to grits mixture. Bake in 1½-quart casserole dish in 325° oven for 1 hour.
Yield: 10 servings
Note: This soufflé can be made ahead and frozen.

Cheese Strata
½ tablespoon margarine
12 slices white bread
3 cups grated sharp Cheddar cheese
2 eggs
2½ cups milk
pinch of salt
pinch of pepper

Grease a 9-by-13-inch casserole dish with margarine. Cut off crusts of bread and place half of bread in bottom of casserole dish. Completely cover with grated cheese. Cover with another layer of bread. Beat together eggs, milk, salt, and pepper. Pour over top of bread and cheese in casserole dish, letting soak through. Put in refrigerator overnight. Bake in 325° oven for about 1 hour. Bake until puffy.
Yield: 10 servings

Perfect Boiled Eggs:
Cover eggs with cool water in pan on stove. Bring to a boil. Immediately turn off heat. Put lid on pan and let stand for 10-15 minutes.

Hemlock Inn Pimento Cheese
1 (4-ounce) jar pimentos, drained
3½ cups grated sharp Cheddar cheese
½ cup mayonnaise
pinch of salt

Cut pimentos in pieces. Mix cheese, pimentos, mayonnaise, and salt in mixing bowl. At medium speed in electric mixer, mix until consistency for easy spreading. More mayonnaise may be added if needed to spread more easily.
Yield: 4 cups

Hemlock Inn Cheese Grits
2 cups cooked coarse-ground grits
½ cup grated sharp Cheddar cheese
¼ cup melted margarine

Mix grits with cheese until well blended. Stir in melted margarine. Put in 1½-quart oblong casserole dish and bake in 350° oven for about 20 minutes or until cheese melts and is hot.
Yield: 10 servings

Scrambled Eggs

approximately ¼ cup vegetable oil
22 eggs
pinch of salt
pinch of pepper

Pour the oil in a skillet with the burner set to medium. In a mixing bowl, beat the eggs well. Pour eggs into skillet. Stir constantly. After approximately 1 minute, before the eggs look done, remove the skillet from the stove. Continue to stir the eggs and let the eggs set for 2–3 minutes before serving. Salt and pepper to taste.

Yield: 15 servings

Lucille's Sausage Egg Soufflé

1 pound mild bulk pork sausage
6 eggs
2 cups milk
1 teaspoon salt
1 teaspoon dry mustard
1 cup grated Cheddar cheese
6 slices white bread, cubed

Crumble and brown sausage. Drain off grease and cool. Mix eggs, milk, salt, and dry mustard, and add to cheese and bread. Add to sausage and stir. Pour into 9-by-13-inch casserole dish and refrigerate overnight. Bake for 45 minutes in 350° oven.

Yield: 6 servings

Hemlock Inn Grits

½ teaspoon salt
1 cup coarse-ground grits

Pour 4 cups water into heavy boiler and add salt. Bring water to boil and add grits. Immediately turn heat down to very slow cooking. Stir very often since grits stick easily. Cook for about 45 minutes.

Yield: 10 servings

So many people ask about our scrambled eggs. We do not add milk or cream to them. I think that the secret to good scrambled eggs is having the oil hot, beating the eggs well, using a black skillet, and taking the eggs off the flame before they look done. They will cook a little more after the heat is off and you have stirred some more. You must stir constantly.

BREADS

Our Heavenly Father, we would truly come unto Thee this new day. We come because of our need and not because of our worth. We pray that somehow we might learn to walk with Thee in a way that is pleasing to Thee. We thank Thee for Thy strength and now for this food. In Jesus' name we ask it. Amen.

Yeast roll step-by-step

Hemlock Inn Yeast Rolls

¾ cup scalded milk
1 generous tablespoon yeast
⅛ cup sugar
3 tablespoons vegetable oil
1 egg
3½ cups all-purpose flour
1 teaspoon salt
½ cup melted butter or margarine

Put milk on to warm. Put yeast and ¼ cup lukewarm water in bowl. Put sugar and oil in mixing bowl. Slightly beat egg in small bowl. Mix milk, yeast, and egg with sugar and oil. Mix well. Put in ½ cup flour and add salt. Beat until air bubbles appear. Gradually add more flour until stiff (using almost all remaining 3 cups flour). Cover with melted butter, and let dough rise until double. Do not let it set after dough rises. Roll out dough and cut out rolls (see photo 1). Fold one end over completely to the opposite side and pinch down (see photos 2 and 3). Butter and let rise again (see photo 4). Bake at 500°–550° for about 10 minutes.

Yield: 36 rolls

Note: We use White Lily flour. To make whole-wheat rolls, replace all-purpose flour with a ratio of one-third whole-wheat flour to two-thirds white flour.

Scalded Milk

Heat the milk to 180°. At this temperature, the milk should just begin to come to a light froth; you will see around the edges of the pan where tiny bubbles form. This point can be determined visually or with a thermometer and can be done in a double boiler or, if you pay close attention, over direct heat. You can also scald milk in a glass bowl in your microwave oven, checking it every 15–20 seconds. To prevent scorching, be sure to stir the milk as it heats.

Corn Muffins

2 eggs
2 cups self-rising cornmeal
¼ cup self-rising flour
1 teaspoon sugar
¼ cup melted butter or margarine
1 cup milk

Beat eggs slightly. Add other ingredients and mix well until no lumps. Pour into greased muffin pans and bake in 400° oven for 15–20 minutes.
Yield: 18 muffins

Cook's Refrigerated Rolls

4 tablespoons yeast
4 eggs
¾ cup shortening
¾ cup sugar
4 teaspoons salt
16 cups all-purpose flour

Mix yeast in 1 cup warm water. Beat eggs well and set aside. Mix together 4 cups hot water, shortening, sugar, and salt. Let cool to lukewarm. Add yeast and eggs. Stir in about 16 cups flour or enough to make soft dough. Store in refrigerator at least 1 hour, up to 8 hours. When ready to bake, pinch out enough dough to make one roll and place on baking sheet. Let rise. Bake in preheated 500° oven about 10 minutes.
Yield: 72 rolls

Ginger Muffins

1¼ cups shortening
1 cup sugar
4 eggs
4 cups all-purpose flour
2 teaspoons ground ginger
2 teaspoons baking soda
½ teaspoon salt
½ teaspoon ground cinnamon
1 cup buttermilk
1 cup dark corn syrup

Cream shortening and sugar. Add eggs one at a time. Mix dry ingredients and add to shortening mixture, alternating with buttermilk and syrup. Mix well until smooth. Cover bowl before placing in refrigerator or bake immediately. Pour batter in greased muffin tins. Bake in 400° oven for 10–12 minutes. The uncooked mixture will keep indefinitely in refrigerator; just spoon out mixture as needed. Do not stir again.
Yield: 48 muffins

Palace Spoon Bread

2 cups cornmeal
1 teaspoon salt
3 eggs, beaten
¼ cup butter or margarine, melted
2 cups milk

Boil 4 cups water, and sprinkle cornmeal and salt into boiling water. Stir for 1 minute. Remove from heat. Add eggs and beat well. Add melted butter. Add milk and whip until well blended. Pour into a well-greased 1½-quart baking dish. Bake in 350° oven for 40–50 minutes. Test for doneness in center of bread. Serve immediately.
Yield: 6 servings

Hemlock Inn Biscuits

6 cups self-rising flour
3 tablespoons baking powder
1½ cups shortening
2–2¼ cups buttermilk

Sift flour and baking powder together into bowl. Cut in shortening until mixture is the consistency of coarse crumbs. Blend in just enough buttermilk with fork until dough leaves sides of bowl (too much makes dough too sticky too handle and not enough makes biscuits dry). Knead gently 10–12 strokes on a lightly floured surface. Split dough in half, rolling each half until about ½-inch thick. Cut out biscuits without twisting cutter and brush buttermilk on tops. Bake at 500° until golden brown— approximately 8–10 minutes.
Yield: 96 small biscuits
Note: We use White Lily flour and Crisco.

Emily's Jalapeño Corn Bread

2 eggs, beaten
½ cup vegetable oil
1 (6-ounce) can cream-style corn
2 medium onions, chopped
½ green bell pepper, chopped
2 cups self-rising cornmeal
1 cup buttermilk
1 jalapeño pepper, chopped
½ cup grated sharp Cheddar cheese, divided

Grease 9-by-13-inch baking dish. Sprinkle with cornmeal. Mix together eggs, oil, corn, onion, bell pepper, cornmeal, buttermilk, and jalapeño pepper. Pour half of batter in pan. Sprinkle half of grated cheese over batter. Pour remaining batter over cheese, and then add remaining cheese. Bake at 400°–450° oven until brown, about 45 minutes to 1 hour.
Yield: 8 servings

Mildred was one of our cooks in the 1980s.

Corn Bread

1 egg
2 cups self-rising cornmeal
¼ cup self-rising flour
¼ cup melted butter or margarine
2 cups buttermilk

Beat egg slightly. Add other ingredients and mix well until no lumps. Pour into well-greased, hot black skillet. Bake in 450° oven for 25–30 minutes.
Yield: 10 servings
Note: For "lighter" corn bread, leave out the egg.

Mil's Pineapple Muffins

4 cups self-rising flour
3 teaspoons baking soda
4 cups cornmeal
8 tablespoons brown sugar
8 eggs
6 cups buttermilk
2 cups drained, crushed pineapple
1 cup bacon grease or vegetable oil
¼ cup bacon bits

Sift flour, baking soda, cornmeal, and sugar together. Slightly beat eggs and add eggs, buttermilk, pineapple, and bacon grease to flour mixture. Mix until smooth. Grease muffin pans well and fill ⅔ full of mixture. Top with bacon bits. Bake in 425° oven for 15–20 minutes.
Yield: 48 muffins

Ruth Kelley's Egg Bread

1½ cups scalded milk (see page 45)
1½ cups white cornmeal
1 teaspoon salt
2 tablespoons melted shortening
2½ teaspoons baking powder
1 egg, beaten

Mix all ingredients together until well blended. Grease 10-inch black skillet, and pour in batter. Bake in 400° oven for 20 minutes.

Yield: 8 servings

Protein Bread

4 tablespoons yeast
4 teaspoons sugar
2 teaspoons salt
2 teaspoons apple cider vinegar
1 cup soy all-purpose flour
3 cups gluten all-purpose flour
5 cups whole-wheat all-purpose flour

Dissolve yeast in 4 cups warm water. Add sugar, salt, and vinegar. Slowly add soy and gluten flour; then add whole-wheat flour. Mix slowly until dough stiffens and does not stick. Knead well for about 5 minutes. Put in four bread pans. Let dough rise in warm place. Bake in 325° oven for about 1 hour or until brown.

Yield: 4 loaves or 48 servings

Mil's Applesauce Muffins

2 cups sugar
4 cups all-purpose flour
1 teaspoon ground cloves
3 teaspoons ground cinnamon
2 teaspoons ground allspice
2 teaspoons baking soda
2 eggs
2 cups applesauce
16 tablespoons margarine, melted
1 teaspoon vanilla extract
1 cup chopped pecans or walnuts

Sift together all dry ingredients. Mix eggs, applesauce, margarine, vanilla, and nuts together, and add to dry ingredients. Mix until smooth. Bake in greased muffin pans in 425° oven 15–20 minutes. The batter can be stored in a covered bowl in the refrigerator for 2 months and used as needed.

Yield: 48 muffins

Louise's Banana Bread

12 tablespoons butter or margarine
1½ cups sugar
1½ cups mashed banana
2 eggs, well beaten
2 cups all-purpose flour
1 teaspoon baking soda
¾ teaspoon salt
½ cup buttermilk
1 cup chopped walnuts or pecans
1 teaspoon vanilla extract

Cream butter and sugar. Add mashed bananas. Add remaining ingredients. Mix until smooth. Grease loaf pan and sprinkle with sugar. Add batter to pan. Bake in 325° oven for approximately 1 hour and 15 minutes.
Yield: 1 large loaf or 2 small loaves; 10–12 servings

Louise Abbott and her husband, Gerald, were two of our most faithful guests. They visited the inn for more than 50 years, and after they both retired, they came every month that we were open except August. When we asked why they didn't come in August, Louise told us that their homeowners' insurance and car insurance were due that month. It was then that we realized the inn was part of their household budget. One of their friends asked Louise if they had ownership in the inn, and she replied, "Yes, we do, but we can't get a clear title."

Myrtle's Pumpkin Bread

2½ cups all-purpose flour
2 cups sugar
2 cups canned pumpkin
½ cup vegetable oil
½ teaspoon ground cloves
2 teaspoons baking soda
1 teaspoon ground cinnamon
½ teaspoon salt
½ teaspoon vanilla extract
½ cup chopped pecans

Mix all ingredients together until smooth. Grease and flour two 1-pound coffee cans or two loaf pans. Pour batter into two cans and bake in preheated 350° oven for 1 hour. Turn off oven and leave in oven for 15 minutes. Turn bread out of coffee cans onto cloth when cool.
Yield: 16 servings

Hemlock Bran Muffins

3 cups sugar
5 cups all-purpose flour
1 (15-ounce) box raisin bran cereal
1 teaspoon salt
5 teaspoons baking soda
4 eggs, slightly beaten
4 cups buttermilk
16 tablespoons butter or margarine, melted

Mix dry ingredients together in a large bowl. Mix wet ingredients together and fold into the dry mixture. Place in covered bowl in refrigerator and take out desired amount as needed. Batter will keep for 2 months. Bake at 350° for 25 minutes.
Yield: 48 large muffins
Note: We use Kellogg's Raisin Bran cereal for this recipe.

Mother's Bran Bread

1 cup bran
½ cup sugar
2 teaspoons salt
1 cup shortening
1 (0.25-ounce) envelope yeast (approximately 1 tablespoon)
2 eggs
6 cups all-purpose flour

Mix bran, sugar, salt, shortening, and 1 cup boiling water together. Set aside and cool. In separate bowl, dissolve yeast in 1 cup lukewarm water, and add to bran mixture. Slowly add eggs (room temperature) and flour. Mix until smooth. Let dough rise until double. Punch down. Divide in quarters and place in four well-greased bread pans that have been floured. Do not preheat oven. Bake in 325° oven for 40 minutes.
Yield: 4 loaves or 48 servings

Hemlock Dressing

2 cups chopped celery
1¼ cups chopped onions
1 cup vegetable oil
4 cups crumbled corn bread
3 cups large, dry breadcrumbs
2 teaspoons salt
¼ teaspoon pepper
1 teaspoon poultry seasoning
6 cups chicken broth
4 eggs, beaten

Sauté celery and onions in oil until celery is tender but not brown. Mix together corn bread, breadcrumbs, salt, pepper, poultry seasoning, and chicken broth. Allow crumbs to soften. Add eggs to bread mixture. Add celery and onions. Turn into buttered 9-by-13-inch pan and bake in 400° oven about 30 minutes.
Yield: 12 servings

Sweet Potato Muffins

2¼ cups all-purpose flour
2¼ cups whole-wheat all-purpose flour
6 teaspoons baking powder
1½ teaspoons ground cinnamon
1½ teaspoons ground nutmeg
1½ teaspoons ground cloves
1 cup sugar
2 cups cooked, mashed sweet potatoes
1½ cups milk
3 eggs
¾ cup melted butter or margarine
1½ cups raisins

Sift together flours, baking powder,
cinnamon, nutmeg, cloves, and sugar.
Mix together sweet potatoes, milk,
eggs, margarine, and raisins. Add to
dry ingredients. Mix until smooth.
Put in well-greased muffin pans.
Bake in 400° oven for 20 minutes.
Yield: 48 muffins

Irene's Zucchini Walnut Bread

1 cup black walnuts, divided
4 eggs
2 cups sugar
1 cup vegetable oil
3½ cups all-purpose flour
1½ teaspoons baking soda
1½ teaspoons salt
¾ teaspoon baking powder
1 teaspoon ground cinnamon, divided
2 cups packed grated zucchini
1 cup raisins
1 teaspoon vanilla extract
¼ cup brown sugar

Chop walnuts into medium pieces.
Reserve ¼ cup walnuts. Beat eggs
and gradually add sugar, and then oil.
Combine flour, baking soda, salt,
baking powder, and ½ teaspoon
cinnamon. Add to sugar mixture
alternately with zucchini, raisins, and
walnuts. Add vanilla. Pour into two
greased and floured loaf pans. Sprinkle
brown sugar, remaining ¼ cup walnuts,
and ½ teaspoon cinnamon on top
before baking. Bake on lowest rack in
350° oven for 55 minutes. Let stand 10
minutes. Turn onto wire racks to cool.
Yield: 2 loaves or 18–20 servings

Irene was another one
of our cooks in the
1980s.

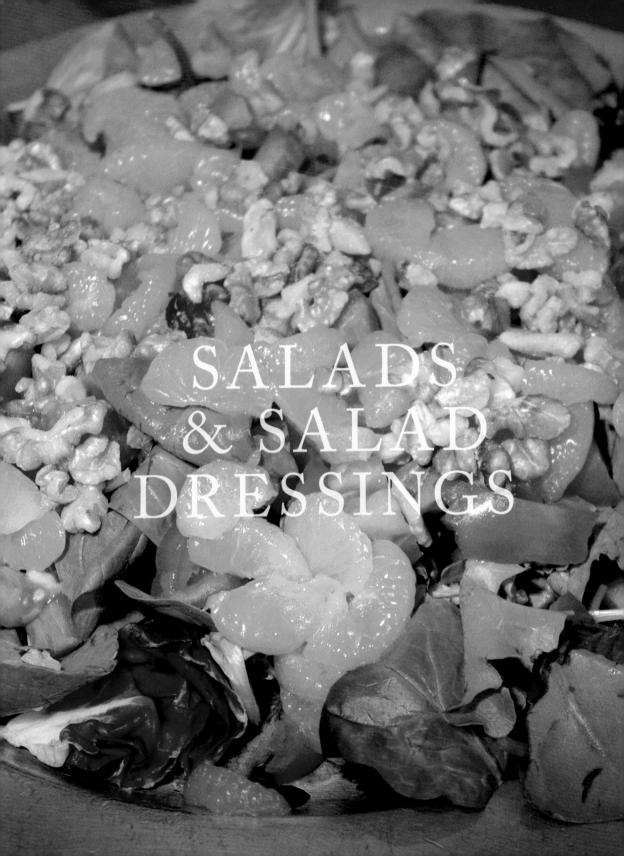

SALADS & SALAD DRESSINGS

Our Heavenly Father, we have already felt Thy presence this Sunday, and for this we are so grateful. We thank Thee for a day that we might wait on Thee, and we pray that this would be a special day and that Thou would speak to us especially. We thank Thee for Thy mercy and this lovely day, and now for this food. In Jesus' name we ask it. Amen.

Rhubarb-Strawberry Salad

1 (6-ounce) package strawberry gelatin
1 (10-ounce) package frozen strawberries, thawed
1¼ cup Rhubarb (see note below)
pinch of salt

Mix gelatin with 1 cup boiling water. Add strawberries and Rhubarb to gelatin mixture. Add salt and pour into 3-quart ring mold. Refrigerate until firm, about 3 hours. Turn mold onto serving plate.
Yield: 12 servings
Note: You can purchase frozen rhubarb in some stores or online; see page 78 for directions on how to prepare fresh or frozen rhubarb for use in this recipe.

Velda's Pear Salad

1 cup grated carrots
juice and grated rind of 1 lemon
½ cup sugar
48 canned pear halves
leaves from two heads of lettuce

Combine first 3 ingredients. Let stand overnight. Drain well. Fill pear halves with one teaspoon of carrot mixture and serve on lettuce.
Yield: 48–50 servings

Beulah's Kraut Salad

1 (16-ounce) can (2 cups) shredded sauerkraut
⅓ cup vegetable oil
½ cup sugar
1 cup sliced onion
1 cup chopped celery
1 cup chopped green bell pepper
1 (3-ounce) can whole pimentos

Drain sauerkraut very well. Mix together oil and sugar and add to kraut. Mix onion, celery, bell pepper, and pimentos and add to sauerkraut mixture. Refrigerate at least 6 hours before serving.
Yield: 12 servings

Jane's Cherry Gelatin Salad

1 (16-ounce) can (2 cups) sour (tart) cherries
1 (16-ounce) can (2 cups) crushed pineapple
1 (6-ounce) package cherry gelatin
1 tablespoon unflavored gelatin
1 orange peel, grated
1 lemon peel, grated
½ cup chopped pecans
pinch of salt
¾ cup sugar

Drain cherries and crushed pineapple well, and reserve juices. Mix cherry gelatin with 1 cup boiling water. Combine cherry and pineapple juice, and add 1 cup of the juice to the gelatin mixture; discard the rest. Mix unflavored gelatin with 1 tablespoon cold water and add to hot cherry gelatin mixture. Mix orange and lemon rinds, pecans, salt, and sugar. Add to gelatin mixture and mix all ingredients together. Put in large 9-by-13-inch glass baking dish. Let set in refrigerator until firm, approximately 2 hours.

Yield: 12 servings

Lyday's Calico Salad

1 (16-ounce) can (2 cups) cut green beans
1 (16-ounce) can (2 cups) cut wax beans
1 (16-ounce) can (2 cups) kidney beans
½ cup chopped red onion
½ cup chopped green bell pepper
¾ cup sugar
⅔ cup white vinegar
⅓ cup olive oil
1 teaspoon salt
¾ teaspoon pepper

Drain beans and mix together. Add chopped onion and bell pepper. Combine sugar, vinegar, oil, salt, and pepper and add to bean mixture. Refrigerate overnight. Take out of refrigerator 1 hour before serving.

Yield: 12 servings

Crunchy Cauliflower Salad

1 medium head cauliflower
1 cup sliced radishes
½ cup sliced green onions
1 (8-ounce) can sliced water chestnuts, drained
¾ cup sour cream
¾ cup mayonnaise
2 tablespoons caraway seeds
1 (0.37-ounce) package buttermilk ranch salad dressing mix

Wash cauliflower, and break into florets. Combine cauliflower and next 3 ingredients in a medium bowl; toss gently. Stir together remaining ingredients. Pour over vegetables and stir well. Spoon into serving bowl. Cover and chill 2 hours before serving.

Yield: 8 servings

Broccoli Salad

1 cup mayonnaise
½ cup sugar
¼ cup chopped onion
2 tablespoons white vinegar
2 heads broccoli
1 cup raisins
¼ cup bacon bits

Mix mayonnaise, sugar, onion, and vinegar. Wash broccoli, and break into florets. Toss mayonnaise mixture with broccoli florets and raisins. Sprinkle bacon bits on top.

Yield: 10 servings

Applesauce Salad

1 (16-ounce) jar (2 cups) applesauce
1 (6-ounce) package cherry gelatin
1 (8-ounce) can crushed pineapple, drained
pinch of salt
½ cup chopped pecans

Mix applesauce and cherry gelatin together in heavy saucepan. Bring to boil. Stir in crushed pineapple, salt, and pecans. Put in 9-by-13-inch glass baking dish and refrigerate until firm, approximately 2 hours.

Yield: 8 servings

Mil's Orange-Pineapple Salad

1 (16-ounce) can (2 cups) crushed pineapple
1 (6-ounce) package orange gelatin
2 cups buttermilk
1 (8-ounce) container frozen whipped topping

Mix crushed pineapple and gelatin together and put in boiler. Bring slowly to boil. Set aside and let cool. Add buttermilk and fold in whipped topping.

Yield: 12 servings

Emerald Salad

1 (6-ounce) package lime gelatin
1½ cups grated cucumber and rind
2 tablespoons grated onion
1 (8-ounce) container cottage cheese
1 cup mayonnaise
¾ cup slivered almonds

Mix gelatin with ¾ cup boiling water until gelatin dissolves. Let cucumbers drain until they don't even drip. Mix cucumbers and onion with gelatin mixture. Fold in cottage cheese and mayonnaise. Add almonds.

Yield: 12 servings

Jackie's Fruit Salad

1 (16-ounce) can (2 cups) fruit cocktail
¼ head lettuce
1 medium banana
1 teaspoon mayonnaise
1 tablespoon confectioners' sugar

Drain fruit cocktail well. Break up lettuce into bite-size pieces. Cut banana into slices. Toss with mayonnaise and sugar. Serve immediately.
Yield: 4 servings

Apple-Raisin Salad

½ cup raisins
4 Red Delicious apples
2 tablespoons mayonnaise
2 teaspoons lemon juice
pinch of salt

Soak raisins in water for about 10 minutes to plump them. Drain well. Core and cut apples into bite-size pieces; do not peel. Mix with raisins and toss with mayonnaise and lemon juice. Sprinkle with salt. Serve immediately.
Yield: 10 servings

Dear friends voiced strong opinions, mostly negative, when the conversation came up about removing recipes from my mother's original *Recipes from Our Front Porch*. They were shocked that I would remove anything. I referred them to Jackie's Fruit Salad, which made us all laugh. (I actually have wonderful memories of this salad. Try it!) We ended up keeping it and every other recipe in the new edition. We chose to only add, not delete, recipes.

Louise's Luncheon Salad

1 (10.5-ounce) can condensed tomato soup
1½ tablespoons unflavored gelatin
2 (3-ounce) containers cream cheese
1 cup chopped celery
2 tablespoons chopped green bell pepper
1 teaspoon minced onion
½ cup sliced black olives
½ cup broken English walnuts
1 cup mayonnaise

Heat tomato soup; add gelatin softened in ½ cup cold water. Cool. Thoroughly combine remaining ingredients. Add to gelatin mixture. Pour into 3-quart ring mold or 9-by-13-inch baking dish. Chill until firm, about 2 hours.

Yield: 8 servings

Mary Ann's Christmas Salad

1 pound fresh cranberries
2 oranges
2 cups sugar
2 (3-ounce) packages raspberry gelatin
¾ cup whole pecans

Grind cranberries and oranges together (include rind of oranges). Sprinkle sugar over mixture and let set. Mix gelatin with 1 cup boiling water. Do not drain juices; mix gelatin with fruit. Add pecans.

Yield: 12 servings

Waldorf Salad

1 cup chopped Red Delicious apples
2 tablespoons Maraschino cherries
½ cup chopped English walnuts
½ cup diced celery
½ cup mayonnaise

Mix fruit, walnuts, celery, and mayonnaise. Chill 1 hour before serving.

Yield: 4 servings

Hon's Tart Asparagus Salad

2 (0.25-ounce) envelopes
unflavored gelatin
¾ cup sugar
½ cup white vinegar
1 tablespoon minced onion
2 tablespoons lemon juice
1 (10-ounce) can cut green asparagus
1 cup chopped pimentos
1 teaspoon salt
1 (5-ounce) can water chestnuts, sliced
1 cup chopped celery

Mix gelatin and ½ cup cold water together. Bring sugar, vinegar, and 1 cup water to boil. Add to gelatin mixture. Add onion and lemon juice. Add asparagus, pimentos, and salt to mixture. Allow to cool. Add sliced water chestnuts and chopped celery. Chill until firm, about 2 hours.

Yield: 8 servings

Black-Eyed Pea Salad

2 cups black-eyed peas, drained
2 cups shoepeg corn, drained
2 teaspoons dill
1 medium red onion, diced
1 (16-ounce) can Italian diced tomatoes
1 medium cucumber, diced
1 dash cilantro, chopped, if desired
1 (8-ounce) bottle Italian dressing

Mix all ingredients, and marinate for 1 day in refrigerator.

Yield: 12 servings

Hon, also known as Ann Dosser, was one of my mother's best friends. Her daughter Sue is my dear friend, and our sisters are good friends. Miss Ann's mother and my father grew up across the street from one another. Sue and I even called each other "little Hon" when we were young. I guess that my mother and Miss Ann had something special that we wanted. I have a lot of good memories of their laughter in the kitchen.

Dody's 24-Hour Salad

2 (20-ounce) cans crushed pineapple, drained
1 (16-ounce) package miniature marshmallows
½ cup chopped pecans
1 (10-ounce) jar Maraschino cherries, drained
4 cups whipped topping
about 2 cups Topping

Mix pineapple, marshmallows, pecans, and cherries. Fold whipped topping into fruit mixture. Pour into 9-by-13-inch pan. When Topping is cold, pour over salad. Put in refrigerator for 24 hours.
Yield: 20 servings

Topping

3 tablespoons sugar
½ teaspoon salt
1 tablespoon all-purpose flour
3 tablespoons white vinegar
4 eggs
¾ cup milk

Mix sugar, salt, flour, and vinegar together. Beat eggs and add milk. Combine Topping ingredients and cook slowly at low heat until mixture begins to thicken, about 10–15 minutes. Remove from heat and let cool, about 1 hour.
Yield: About 2 cups

Dody's Apricot-Cheese Delight

1 (20-ounce) can crushed pineapple
1 (20-ounce) can cut apricots
2 (3-ounce) packages orange gelatin
1 cup marshmallows
about 4 cups Topping
⅛ cup shredded Cheddar cheese

Drain pineapple and apricots, and reserve juices. Mix gelatin with 2 cups boiling water. Combine pineapple and apricot juices, and add 1 cup of the juice to gelatin mixture; reserve the rest. Add marshmallows and stir until they are melted. When this mixture starts to gel, add pineapple and apricots. After fruit mixture has congealed, spread Topping evenly over it and sprinkle with cheese. Refrigerate for 24 hours before serving.
Yield: 18 servings

Topping

½ cup sugar
3 tablespoons all-purpose flour
1 egg, beaten
¼ teaspoon salt
2 cups grated Cheddar cheese
2 tablespoons butter
1 cup whipped topping

Mix well the first 5 ingredients and add remaining 1 cup pineapple and apricot juice. Cook over low heat until thick, about 10–15 minutes. Remove from heat and add butter. Cool thoroughly. Fold in whipped topping.
Yield: About 4 cups

Lois's Fruit Salad

1 (3-ounce) container cream cheese
½ cup sugar
1 (22-ounce) can cherry pie filling
1 (20-ounce) can pineapple chunks, drained
1 cup chopped pecans
1 cup whipped topping

Cream together cream cheese and sugar. Add pie filling, pineapple, and pecans. Fold whipped topping into mixture. Put in muffin liners in muffin pans and place in freezer overnight or until frozen. Remove from muffin pans and place in airtight container and keep in freezer. The fruit salad will keep for several weeks.
Yield: 12 servings
Note: You may substitute blueberry or strawberry pie filling for the cherry pie filling.

Hemlock Inn Salad Dressing

1 teaspoon salt
6 tablespoons sugar
1 teaspoon garlic powder
½ teaspoon oregano
½ teaspoon basil
½ teaspoon parsley flakes
½ cup white vinegar
1½ cups mayonnaise

Mix all ingredients together until smooth.
Yield: Approximately 2⅔ cups
Note: For French dressing, add 2 tablespoons ketchup.

Warren's Blue Cheese Dressing

1 (16-ounce) container sour cream
2 large cloves garlic
2 (8-ounce) packages blue cheese
2 tablespoons olive oil
1 teaspoon white vinegar
pinch of salt and pepper

Put sour cream in medium-size mixing bowl. Use garlic press to crush garlic, and put crushed garlic and its juice in sour cream. Break blue cheese into small bits and add. Fold in oil and vinegar until smooth. Add salt and pepper to taste.
Yield: 24 servings

Mandarin Orange Salad

2 cups mixed greens
1 cup cherry tomatoes
1 cup mandarin orange slices
¼ cup chopped walnuts
Sylvia's Sweet Dressing, as desired (see opposite page)

Top greens with remaining ingredients, and serve with Sylvia's Sweet Dressing.
Yield: 8–10 servings

Sylvia's Sweet Dressing

1 teaspoon celery seed
1 teaspoon dry mustard
1 teaspoon salt
1 teaspoon paprika
1 teaspoon grated onion
½ cup honey
1 cup vegetable oil
¼ cup tarragon vinegar

Mix all ingredients together well.
Serve over fresh fruit.
Yield: 2 cups
*Note: The dressing is especially good over
fresh grapefruit and avocado.*

Beth's Orange Juice Salad

2 cups mixed greens
½ cup red grapes, sliced
⅛ cup dried cranberries
1 (2.2-ounce) bag slivered almonds
OJ Dressing, as desired

Top greens with remaining ingredients,
and serve with OJ Dressing.
Yield: 8–10 servings

OJ Dressing

1 (6-ounce) can pulp-free frozen
orange juice concentrate
½ cup canola oil
¼ cup apple cider vinegar
3 tablespoons sugar
½ teaspoon dry mustard
¼ teaspoon salt

Mix all ingredients for
dressing together.
Yield: 2 cups

Easy Caesar Dressing

½ cup mayonnaise
¼ cup grated Parmesan cheese
2 tablespoons lemon juice
2 tablespoons water
½ teaspoon pepper
½ teaspoon minced garlic

Mix all ingredients together.
Chill 2 hours.
Yield: 1 cup

Honey Mustard Dressing

¾ cup mayonnaise
3 tablespoons honey
3 tablespoons prepared mustard
1 tablespoon lemon juice
salt
pepper

Mix first 4 ingredients together, and
salt and pepper to taste. Chill 2 hours.
Yield: 1 cup

RELISHES

Our Heavenly Father, we thank Thee for a good night of rest and a new day. Our prayer is that we might do what is pleasing to Thee. We thank Thee for Thy mercy and Thy strength and now for this food. In Jesus' name we ask it. Amen.

Daddy's and Nell's Pickled Eggs

4 cups white vinegar
1 cup water with 1 drop red food coloring, or 1 cup beet juice
1 teaspoon salt
15–18 eggs, hard-boiled

Combine vinegar, water, red food coloring, and salt (we use 1 cup beet juice instead of water and food coloring) and bring to a boil. Place shelled eggs in a gallon glass jar. Pour hot liquid over eggs, and place jar in refrigerator overnight or longer.

Yield: 15–18 eggs

Mashburn's Uncooked Relish

1 cup chopped green bell pepper
1 cup chopped red bell pepper
1 jalapeño pepper, chopped
2 cups shredded cabbage
1 cup chopped onion
2½ tablespoons salt
1 teaspoon celery seed
2 cups white vinegar
2 cups sugar

Drain chopped vegetables. Add salt. Let stand overnight. Drain again very well. Add celery seed, vinegar, and sugar. Store in refrigerator up to 1 month.

Yield: 10 servings

Easy Watermelon Rind Pickles

10 pounds watermelon rind (as weighed after being prepared)
12 pounds sugar
4 cups white vinegar
40 drops clove oil
40 drops cinnamon oil
few drops green food coloring or 1 tablespoon spinach juice

Peel rind and cut into desired pieces. Let stand in cold water for 24 hours. Drain. Cover with fresh water, bring to boil, and let simmer 10 minutes. Drain. Dry on tea towel. Weigh out 10 pounds. Mix sugar, vinegar, clove oil, cinnamon oil, and green food coloring (we use spinach water or any natural green vegetable juice) together and add to rinds. Let stand 24 hours, stirring occasionally. Bring to a boil. Boil 7–10 minutes. Pack in sterilized jars and seal.

Yield: 16 cups

Carrot-Cucumber Relish

**3½ cups coarsely ground unpeeled
cucumbers (approximately 4–6
cucumbers, washed with ends cut off)
1½ cups coarsely ground carrots
(approximately 6 medium carrots,
peeled with ends cut off)
1 cup coarsely ground onions
2 tablespoons salt
2½ cups sugar
1½ cups white vinegar
1½ teaspoons celery seed
1½ teaspoons mustard seed**

Combine ground cucumbers, carrots,
onions, and salt and let stand 3 hours.
Drain well. Combine sugar, vinegar,
celery seed, and mustard seed and bring
to boil. Add vegetables and simmer,
uncovered, for 20 minutes. Seal at once
in sterilized jars.

Yield: 6 cups

Crystal Pickles

**16 cups sliced cucumbers
1 cup salt
2 teaspoons alum baking powder
6 cups white vinegar
8 cups sugar, divided
2 tablespoons pickling spices**

Place cucumbers into container. Pour salt
over them and fill with enough water to
cover them. Let set 7 days, stirring
occasionally (about twice a day).

On the 8th day, pour water off.
Pour enough boiling water to cover the
cucumbers and let stand overnight.

On the 9th day, pour water off.
Add alum to mixture. Pour enough
boiling water over mixture to cover it
and let stand overnight.

On the 10th day, pour water off. Rinse
well. Pour enough boiling water to cover
the cucumbers and let stand overnight.

On the 11th day, pour water off. Rinse
again. Mix vinegar, 6 cups sugar, and
pickling spices, and pour over mixture.
Let set overnight.

On the 12th day, pour vinegar mixture
into pan. Use ½ cup boiling water to
dissolve 1 cup sugar. Add 1 cup dissolved
sugar to vinegar mixture. Pour over
cucumbers and let set overnight.

On the 13th day, pour vinegar mixture
into pan. Use ½ cup boiling water to
dissolve 1 cup sugar. Add 1 cup dissolved
sugar to vinegar mixture. Pour over
cucumbers and let set overnight.

On the 14th day, pour vinegar mixture
into saucepan. Boil. Put cucumber mixture
into sterilized jars. Pour boiling vinegar
mixture over them and seal.

Yield: 12 cups

Bess Perry's Pickles

6 large onions, sliced
16 cups thinly sliced cucumbers
2 green bell peppers, sliced
½ cup salt
2 bulbs garlic
1½ teaspoons celery seed
1½ teaspoons turmeric
2 tablespoons mustard seed
5 cups sugar
2 cups white vinegar

Mix onions, cucumbers, peppers, and salt together. Cover with ice and soak 3 hours. Drain vegetables. Combine remaining ingredients and pour over onions, cucumbers, and peppers. Heat to boiling and seal in sterilized jars.

Yield: 12 cups

Damson Plum Preserves

6 cups damson plums
or 3 pounds ripe plums
5½ cups sugar

Sort and wash plums. Remove pits. Dissolve sugar in 1 cup water and bring to boil. Add plums and boil, stirring gently, to 221° or until fruit is transparent and the syrup is thick. Remove preserves from heat and ladle at once into sterilized jars. Seal.

Yield: 6 cups

Pear Jam

3 pounds ripe soft pears
4½ cups sugar
1 (6-ounce) box powdered fruit pectin

Peel and core pears. Grind thoroughly. Measure sugar into a dry dish and set aside until needed. Measure prepared pears into a 5- or 6-quart kettle. Be sure that you have 3½ cups of pears. Add water, if necessary, to make the 3½ cups. Add pectin, mix until powder is dissolved, and continue stirring until mixture comes to rolling boil. Add sugar and stir constantly. Continue stirring and bring to full rolling boil again. Boil hard for 1 minute. Remove from heat, and skim boiling froth off. Pour quickly into sterilized jars. Seal.

Yield: 6–8 cups

Myrtle's Something Good

2 cups chopped red bell peppers
2 cups chopped green bell peppers
4 cups peeled and chopped
Granny Smith apples
4 cups chopped cabbage
4 cups chopped green tomatoes
4 cups chopped onions
2 tablespoons prepared mustard
4 cups white vinegar
4 cups sugar
2 tablespoons salt

Stir all ingredients, and cook at low
boil for 20 minutes.
Seal in sterilized jars.
Yield: 16 cups

Grape Jelly

4 cups Grape Juice (see recipe at right;
leave out sugar)
3 cups sugar

Pour juice into large container and let
stand in refrigerator for 24–48 hours.
Strain juice again to remove crystals
that will be seen clinging to sides of jar.
Place juice in large kettle. Boil rapidly
for 5 minutes. Add sugar and boil until
it reaches the jelly stage, about 218°–
220° on thermometer. Pour into hot,
sterilized jars and seal.
Yield: 6–8 cups

Grape Juice

Stem blue Concord grapes. Wash grapes and put in kettle with barely enough water to cover grapes. Boil until all seeds are free and juice seems to be cooked out. Drain in a bag and reserve juice. Return juice to kettle and bring to boil. Add ⅓ cup sugar to each 1 quart (4 cups) of juice. Let boil rapidly for 5 minutes. Seal in sterilized jars. Note: If you plan to make jelly from the juice later, do not add sugar when canning the juice.

SOUPS &
SAUCES

Our Heavenly Father, how happy we are to pause and give Thee thanks for this lovely day and for Thy love. We are so grateful that Thou dost care for us and watch over us, and particularly that Thou dost call us by our first name. Thank you for these good friends and now for this food. In Jesus' name we ask it. Amen.

Bean Soup

1 country ham bone
3 medium onions
2 carrots
1 (1-pound) package great northern beans

Put ham bone in heavy boiler with 8 cups water. Cook at high heat until ham falls off bone (about 1 hour). Remove ham bone and set broth aside. Put beans in a boiler with 6 cups water and bring to boil. Set aside beans in their own juice for about 2–3 hours. Chop onions and shred carrots. Add ham broth to bean mixture. Add onions and carrots and bring to boil. Simmer about 2 hours.

Yield: 12 large servings

Quick Veggie Soup

1 pound ground turkey
1 small onion, chopped
1 teaspoon salt
½ teaspoon pepper
1 (29-ounce) can mixed vegetables
1 (28-ounce) can diced tomatoes
1 (28-ounce) can kidney beans

Brown turkey and onions. Drain off any grease. Add salt and pepper. Add cans of mixed vegetables, tomatoes, and kidney beans; do not drain the cans. Bring to a boil, and then simmer for 20 minutes.

Yield: 8 servings

Note: We use Veg-all brand.

Vegetable Soup

leftover beef or chicken in its broth
onions
grated carrots
rice
leftover vegetables of any kind
2 cups tomatoes

Our vegetable soup was once made from leftover meat and vegetables. We always had chopped onions, grated carrots, rice, and cooked tomatoes and then added anything else we had during the week. Usually, we added corn, lima beans, okra, celery, green beans, or parsley, but don't go out and buy something for your soup. The more you can use what you have, the better your soup. Salt and pepper to taste. Most of the time your meat and/or vegetables are already seasoned, so be careful that you don't add too much. Let simmer for about 2 hours.

Things have changed so much over the years. For instance, we are no longer able to use our leftover food, but this is still a great idea for you at home.

Yield: 12–40 servings

Veggie Chowder Soup

2 small potatoes, chopped
1 small onion, chopped
4 tablespoons butter
1–2 stems broccoli, chopped
1 (12-ounce) can evaporated milk
1 (16-ounce) block processed cheese, chopped
1 (10.75-ounce) can cream of celery soup
1 (10.75-ounce) can cream of mushroom soup
1 (10.75-ounce) can cream of chicken soup
about 4 cups (3 soup cans) whole milk
1 (15-ounce) can whole corn
1 (4-ounce) jar diced pimentos

Sauté potatoes and onion in butter. Add broccoli. Meanwhile, microwave evaporated milk and cheese 1 minute at a time. Stir after every minute until no lumps (about 4–5 minutes). To potatoes, onion, and broccoli, add the remaining ingredients except cheese mixture. Warm thoroughly and add cheese mixture.

Yield: 12 servings

Note: This is great to make in an electric cooking pot. We use Velveeta processed cheese product.

Cream of Pimento Soup

1 (4-ounce) jar diced pimentos
2 tablespoons butter
2½ tablespoons all-purpose flour
1 (14.25-ounce) can chicken broth
1½ cups half-and-half
2 teaspoons grated onion
½ teaspoon salt
¼ teaspoon hot sauce

Place pimentos (do not drain) in electric blender, and blend until smooth. Melt butter in heavy saucepan over low heat. Add flour and stir until smooth. Cook 1 minute. Add chicken broth and half and half gradually. Cook over medium heat until thick and bubbly. Stir in pimentos, onion, salt, and hot sauce. Cook over low heat until heated thoroughly.

Yield: 8 servings

Mil's Spaghetti Sauce

1 pound ground beef
1 (6-ounce) can tomato paste
1 (8-ounce) can tomato sauce
½ cup finely chopped onion
1½ cups water
2 teaspoons brown gravy mix
1 fresh crushed garlic clove
2 teaspoons Worcestershire sauce
2 teaspoons sugar
1 teaspoon oregano
1 teaspoon basil
½ teaspoon salt
½ teaspoon pepper
¼ cup grated Parmesan cheese

Sauté beef and add to other ingredients. Simmer very slowly in open kettle or a saucepan for 1½–2 hours. Stir often.

Yield: 8 servings

Georgia's Spaghetti Sauce

1 tablespoon chopped onion
1 tablespoon vegetable oil
1 pound ground beef
2 cups tomato sauce
1 cup tomato paste
1 teaspoon salt
1 teaspoon pepper
1 tablespoon Worcestershire sauce
1 tablespoon brown gravy mix
1 garlic clove or 1 teaspoon garlic salt

Brown onion in oil. Add ground beef and cook but don't brown, about 5 minutes. Put meat and onion mixture in large pot, and add tomato sauce and tomato paste. Add salt, pepper, Worcestershire, brown gravy mix, and garlic. Simmer on low heat for at least 3 hours.

Yield: 10 servings

Beef Gravy

1 cup juice reserved from cooked roast
¼ cup all-purpose flour

Pour hot juices from cooking beef roast into skillet. Add flour slowly, stirring constantly over medium heat. Whisk until well blended. Add 3 cups water and cook slowly until gravy browns and thickens, about 15 minutes.

Yield: 2 cups

Georgia and her husband, Raymond, owned the inn in the mid-1960s.

Barbecue Sauce

4 tablespoons butter or margarine
½ cup apple cider vinegar
1 garlic clove, crushed
⅓ cup lemon juice
1 teaspoon grated lemon rind
½ teaspoon cayenne pepper
½ cup vegetable oil
2 tablespoons ketchup
1½ tablespoons Worcestershire sauce
1 tablespoon salt
½ teaspoon pepper

Mix all ingredients together well, until smooth. Bring mixture to boil. Turn down heat and simmer for 45 minutes.

Yield: 10 servings

74

FRUITS &
VEGETABLES

Our Heavenly Father, we are blessed because we know Thee. We lift our hearts to Thee in praise and give thanks for this good day, for Thy mercy, and especially for these friends, and now for this food. In Jesus' name we pray. Amen.

Curried Fruit

½ cup butter, melted
½ cup brown sugar
2 teaspoons curry powder
2 cups canned peach halves
2 cups canned pear halves
2 cups canned pineapple tidbits
2 cups canned apricot halves

Pour melted butter into casserole dish, and place brown sugar and curry powder in dish. Arrange fruit on top of mixture. Bake in 350° oven for 45 minutes to 1 hour.
Yield: 12 servings

Rhubarb

4 cups cut rhubarb
pinch of salt
1 cup sugar

Wash and trim off ends of rhubarb. Peel like celery. Cut into bite-size pieces and place into small roaster. Sprinkle salt and sugar on top. Place in 350° oven and bake for about 1 hour or until well done.
Yield: 8–10 servings
Note: Some people like rhubarb to be the consistency of applesauce; others like it not so well done. There are many varieties of rhubarb: strawberry, cherry, crimson, and several others. It's fun to see different varieties growing; each has its own color.

E.J.'s Cranberries

2 cups sugar
4 cups orange juice
4 cups fresh cranberries
2 cups English walnuts

Bring sugar and orange juice to boil. Add cranberries and cook 6 minutes. Take off heat, add walnuts, and let cool.
Yield: 12 servings
Note: Try this fabulous recipe at Thanksgiving.

Baked Apples

6 baking apples (see note below)
½ cup sugar
2 teaspoons cinnamon
¼ cup melted margarine

Wash, core, and quarter apples. Do not peel apples. Mix sugar and cinnamon together. Place apples in deep baking pan and sprinkle sugar mixture over them. Pour margarine on top. Cover. Bake in 400° oven for about 1 hour.
Yield: 8 servings
Note: Any good baking apple will do. We use Wolf River or Pippin when we can get them. However, the season for these two apples is short; we use any firm, good apple that we can get during the year.

Doris's Sherried Fruit

1 (16-ounce) can sliced pineapple
1 (16-ounce) can peach halves
1 (16-ounce) can pear halves
1 (16-ounce) can apricot halves
1 (16-ounce) jar spiced apple rings
8 tablespoons butter
1½ cups sugar
2 tablespoons all-purpose flour
1 cup cooking sherry

Drain all fruits. Cut pineapple and peach halves in half and arrange all fruit in layers in large, medium-shallow casserole dish. In double boiler, heat butter, sugar, flour, and sherry over boiling water. Stir constantly until about as thick as cream, about 10 minutes. Pour over fruit and let stand in refrigerator overnight. Bake in 350° oven about 20 minutes or until thoroughly heated and bubbly.

Yield: 12 servings

Note: This fruit is especially good with roast loin of pork, ham, or poultry.

Doris Tyson and her husband, A. R., loved the Hemlock Inn. She knew the original owners and spent more time here than anybody. She also referred and brought more people to the inn than anyone else. The Tysons led hikes and helped guests plan their day's activities. They would trim the boxwoods and do countless projects. However, one thing that Doris never did, or could do, was cook. This fruit salad is her only contribution to this cookbook and, as you notice, requires little cooking. In her later years, she often told whoever would listen that she once owned the inn (though she never did). One thing is for certain: She encouraged and assisted all the owners over a span of 50-plus years. Simply put, there was no one quite like Doris. She passed away at the age of 101.

Miz Frankie's Apricot Casserole

4 cups apricots, drained and mashed
2 ¼ cups (1½ tubes) butter snack
crackers, crushed
1 cup brown sugar
8 tablespoons butter, melted

In round casserole dish, place mashed apricots and layer cracker crumbs and brown sugar on top. Pour melted butter over casserole. Bake at 350° for 20–25 minutes until bubbly.

Yield: 6–8 servings

Note: We use Ritz crackers.

Harriett's Scalloped Pineapple

1 cup sugar
8 tablespoons butter
1 (16-ounce) can pineapple chunks
2 eggs
½ cup milk
½ cup pineapple juice
10 slices fresh white bread, cubed

Mix all ingredients together and bake in 9-by-13-inch greased pan in 375° oven for 30–40 minutes.

Yield: 10 servings

> **"Miz Frankie"** was Frank Calhoun's mother. Frank worked in our office for many years.

Apple and Carrot Casserole

3 cups canned apples
½ cup sugar
4 tablespoons butter or margarine,
melted
1 cup peeled, sliced, and boiled carrots,
drained

Add apples, sugar, and melted butter or margarine to carrots. Cover and bake in 1½-quart casserole dish in 350° oven for 20 minutes.

Yield: 8 servings

Velda's Carrot-Pineapple Posh

3 cups sliced carrots
1 teaspoon salt
1 (20-ounce) can crushed pineapple
with juice
1 cup white raisins
½ cup packed light brown sugar
juice of ½ lemon

Cook carrots in boiling salted water until slightly tender, about 15 minutes. Combine carrots with other ingredients in a well-buttered 1½-quart casserole dish. Bake in 350° oven for 1 hour.

Yield: 8 servings

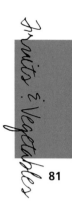

Velda's Crisp Carrot Casserole

**8 large carrots, peeled and sliced,
or 1 (20-ounce) package frozen carrots
¼ cup chopped onion
⅓ cup sugar
salt
pepper
½ cup chopped celery
½ cup mayonnaise**

Put carrots in saucepan with the onion and sugar in just enough water to cover. Cook until carrots are tender, about 15 minutes. Pour off water, and add salt and pepper to taste. Add remaining ingredients. Place in buttered casserole dish and bake at 350° for 30 minutes.
Yield: 12 servings

Velda's Carrot Custard

**2 cups carrots, peeled and sliced
2 eggs
1½ cups milk
½ teaspoon salt
4 tablespoons butter or margarine, melted
1 teaspoon sugar
1 cup grated sharp Cheddar cheese
1 cup breadcrumbs
⅛ teaspoon paprika**

Boil carrots in salted water about 15 minutes and then purée them. Beat eggs and mix together with milk, salt, butter or margarine, and sugar. Add cheese and carrots. Add breadcrumbs and mix. Place in greased 1½-quart casserole and bake for about 30 minutes in 350° oven. Sprinkle paprika on top.
Yield: 10 servings

Velda Woody and her husband, W. H., first came to the inn in the early 1970s when they built a cottage on the inn's property and, for 17 years, stayed for the entire inn season (mid-April through the end of October). Retired from the railroad, W. H. was a hiker, and Velda enjoyed needlework. Occasionally Velda would bring my mom a new recipe and say something such as, "Ella Jo, this might fit into the menu on Thursday." Mom would just laugh and say to the cooks, "Velda needs a change!" Well-deserved for someone who ate dinner with us every night! You will find Velda's recipes scattered throughout the cookbook. W. H., on the other hand, had only two requests: chocolate cake and chocolate pie, preferably every other night!

Fruits & Vegetables

Peg's Carrots

2 pounds (4 cups) carrots,
peeled and sliced
1 medium red onion
1 (11.75-ounce) can tomato soup
½ cup vegetable oil
½ cup apple cider vinegar
½ cup brown sugar
1 teaspoon dry mustard
pinch of salt
pinch of pepper
pinch of garlic powder
2 teaspoons Worcestershire sauce

Boil carrots in salted water until tender,
about 15 minutes; drain and cool. Slice
onion. Mix together tomato soup,
vegetable oil, vinegar, brown sugar, dry
mustard, salt, pepper, and garlic.
Simmer for 12 minutes. Add
Worcestershire sauce and let cool.
Make alternate layers of carrots and
onion rings and pour sauce over them.
Refrigerate and let stand several hours.
This recipe will keep 2 weeks in
refrigerator and may be served cold or
hot. If served cold, let stand at room
temperature for 1 hour before serving.
Yield: 10 servings

Okra Fritters

1 cup self-rising cornmeal
1 (10-ounce) package frozen okra
8 cups vegetable oil for deep-frying

Combine cornmeal and sufficient water
(about ⅛ cup) to form a thick batter.
Cut frozen okra in small bite-size
pieces and stir in batter. Drop by
spoonful into hot oil and deep fry
until golden brown, about 5 minutes,
on high heat. Drain on rack
and serve hot.
Yield: 16 servings

Corn Fritters

1¾ cups self-rising flour
pinch of salt
1 teaspoon sugar
2 eggs
½ cup milk
2 tablespoons margarine, melted
1 (16-ounce) can whole-kernel corn
4 cups vegetable oil for deep-frying

Sift together flour, salt, and sugar.
Beat eggs well and add milk and
melted margarine. Drain corn well
and add to milk and egg mixture,
then add dry ingredients. Drop by
teaspoonfuls into hot oil and deep-fry
until golden brown, about 5 minutes,
on high heat. Drain on rack and
serve hot.
Yield: 24 servings
*Note: Bananas, chopped apples, or pine-
apple can be substituted for corn.*

> May was Mrs. Haynie's best friend. They spent countless hours creating recipes in the kitchen together.

Apple Fritters

6 Red Delicious apples
1 cup self-rising flour
1 tablespoon sugar
4 cups vegetable oil for deep-frying
2 tablespoons sugar, divided

Wash and core apples and slice into ¼-inch pieces. Mix flour, 1 tablespoon sugar, and about ⅛ cup water together. Dip apple slices into thin batter and drop into hot oil until golden brown. Drain and sprinkle with remaining sugar.

Yield: 24 servings

May's Casserole

6 slices white bread
2 cups canned whole tomatoes
½ teaspoon salt
¼ teaspoon pepper
1 tablespoon finely chopped onion
3 eggs
1¼ cups milk
1 cup grated sharp Cheddar cheese

Line bottom of buttered casserole dish with bread slices. Spread drained tomatoes over bread. Add salt, pepper, and onion on top of bread and tomatoes. Beat eggs well and add milk. Pour over bread and tomato mixture. Add grated cheese to top. Bake in 350° oven for 1 hour.

Yield: 10 servings

Fried Onion Rings

2 medium-size Bermuda onions
½ cup all-purpose flour
½ teaspoon salt
4 cups vegetable oil

Slice onions into ¼-inch pieces. Mix flour, salt, and ½ cup water together to make batter. Dip onion rings into batter and fry in hot oil (preheated to 350°) for 1–2 minutes or until golden. Drain on paper towels and serve while hot.

Yield: 6 servings

Dot's Vidalia Onion Pie

2²/₃ tablespoons margarine, divided
20–24 saltine crackers, crushed, divided
1 medium Vidalia onion
²/₃ cup grated sharp Cheddar cheese
1 cup White Sauce

Melt margarine and pour half into the crushed crackers (reserve enough cracker crumbs to sprinkle on top). Blend well. Press cracker crumbs into pie pan. Slice the onion thin and sauté in remaining margarine until tender but not brown. Place onions on the piecrust. Add cheese to White Sauce and heat until cheese has melted. Then pour White Sauce over onions. Sprinkle a few cracker crumbs on top, and bake in 350° oven for about 15 minutes.

Yield: 8 servings

White Sauce

1 tablespoon butter
1 tablespoon all-purpose flour
pinch of salt
1 cup milk

In heavy saucepan, melt butter. Stir in flour and salt, and slowly add milk. Stir constantly with whisk until thick.

Yield: 1 cup

Note: The White Sauce can also be used with chipped beef on toast.

For those of you who don't know about Vidalia onions, let me tell you a little about them. There's a small town in southeast Georgia named Vidalia. The farmers in that area produce an onion that is not only big, healthy, and juicy but also delicious in taste. The residents of Vidalia attribute the success of this onion to the local soil. No place else in the world, so they say, will this onion grow! And I agree—it is delicious. The season for it is so short—usually just June—so those of us who have learned to love them rush out to a nearby Georgia fruit stand that gets a few sacks each year.

Herbed Tomatoes

4 cups canned diced tomatoes
½ teaspoon basil
½ teaspoon oregano
¼ cup brown sugar
1 teaspoon salt
$^1/_8$ teaspoon pepper
$^1/_8$ teaspoon allspice
$^1/_8$ teaspoon cloves
10–12 saltine crackers

Mix together tomatoes, basil, oregano, brown sugar, salt, pepper, allspice, and cloves. Simmer 45 minutes. Break up crackers in serving dish, and pour tomato mixture over them.

Yield: 10 servings

Harvard Beets

$^2/_3$ cup sugar
4 teaspoons cornstarch
½ cup apple cider vinegar
2½ cups canned sliced beets;
reserve ½ cup juice
2 tablespoons margarine

Combine sugar and cornstarch. Stir sugar mixture into vinegar and ½ cup beet juice. Stir over low heat until thickened. Add drained beets and margarine. Heat slowly, about 45 minutes.

Yield: 10 servings

Spinach-Artichoke Casserole

2 (10-ounce) packages frozen spinach
1 (8-ounce) container cream cheese
8 tablespoons butter or margarine
1 (12.75-ounce) can artichokes
1 teaspoon lemon juice
Worcestershire sauce to taste
salt and pepper to taste
½ cup breadcrumbs

Cook frozen spinach according to directions on package. Drain spinach and return to pan; add cream cheese and butter to pan so that they will melt into spinach. Put artichokes on bottom of buttered casserole dish or individual ramekins. Add lemon juice, Worcestershire sauce, salt, and pepper to spinach mixture and put over artichokes. Sprinkle with breadcrumbs and dot with butter. Bake 25 minutes at 350°.

Yield: 6–8 servings

Velda's French Beets

2 teaspoons minced onion
2 teaspoons chopped green bell pepper
2 teaspoons dry parsley
1 teaspoon lemon juice or
apple cider vinegar
1 (10-ounce) can French-style
julienne beets

Mix all ingredients together; heat slowly for 45 minutes and serve.

Yield: 4 servings

Asparagus Casserole

1 (11.75-ounce) can asparagus soup
2 eggs
½ cup powdered milk
juice of 1 lemon
½ teaspoon salt
¼ teaspoon pepper
½ teaspoon onion powder
3 eggs, hard-boiled
½ cup breadcrumbs, divided
1 (16-ounce) can cut asparagus
¼ cup grated sharp Cheddar cheese
1 tablespoon butter

Mix soup, eggs, powdered milk, lemon juice, salt, pepper, and onion powder together. Chop the hard-boiled eggs and add half of breadcrumbs. Add to soup mixture. In casserole dish pour soup mixture and put asparagus on top. Sprinkle grated cheese on top and add remaining breadcrumbs. Dot with butter. Bake in 350° oven until brown, about 20 minutes.

Yield: 8 servings

Cranberry Casserole

2 cups unpeeled raw apples, chopped
2 cups fresh cranberries
1¼ cups sugar
½ cup brown sugar
$^{1}/_{3}$ cup chopped pecans
½ cup melted margarine
1½ cups quick oats (dry)
$^{1}/_{3}$ cup all-purpose flour
dash of ground cinnamon

In 2-quart dish, combine apples, cranberries, and white sugar.
Mix brown sugar, pecans, margarine, oats, flour, and cinnamon. Top fruit mixture with brown sugar mixture. Bake at 350° for 1 hour or until lightly browned.

Yield: 12 servings

Note: Serve hot with chicken or turkey.

Velda's Oriental Cabbage

1 green bell pepper
2 stalks celery
2 medium carrots
1 large onion
8 tablespoons melted margarine
1 medium head cabbage, chopped
¾ cup evaporated milk
dash of salt
dash of pepper
1 scant teaspoon sugar

Cut green pepper into strips. Chop celery and carrots thin and slanted. Slice onion into rings. Melt margarine and add vegetables (including cabbage) in a large skillet. Cover and cook over medium heat for 10 minutes. Stir in milk and heat thoroughly. Add salt, pepper, and sugar to taste.
Yield: 8 servings

Irma's Broccoli Casserole

2 cups cooked broccoli
½ cup Thick White Sauce
½ cup mayonnaise
2 teaspoons onion juice
3 eggs, well beaten
dash of salt
dash of pepper

Combine all ingredients and pour into well-greased 1-quart casserole. Set in pan of 2 cups hot water and bake in 350° oven for about 45 minutes.
Yield: 10 servings

Thick White Sauce

1½ tablespoons butter or margarine
1½ tablespoons all-purpose flour
½ cup milk

In saucepan, melt butter over low heat. Stir in flour. Gradually add milk over medium heat, stirring constantly until thick, about 5 minutes.
Yield: ½ cup

Wilted Lettuce

½ head lettuce
2 fresh spring onions
1 tablespoon bacon drippings
salt to taste
1 tablespoon real bacon bits

Cut up lettuce and onions together and place in serving bowl. Heat bacon drippings on high heat. Pour over lettuce and onion mixture. Pour 1 tablespoon water into hot skillet and immediately pour over lettuce. Sprinkle salt on top and toss in bacon bits.
Yield: 8 servings

Favorite Broccoli Casserole

1 (16-ounce) package frozen chopped broccoli
1 (11.75-ounce) can cream of mushroom soup
2 tablespoons grated onion
2 eggs, well beaten
1 cup grated sharp Cheddar cheese
1 cup mayonnaise
½ cup breadcrumbs
4 tablespoons butter, melted

Cook broccoli until tender, according to package directions, and drain. Mix soup, onion, eggs, cheese, and mayonnaise and fold in thoroughly. Layer broccoli and sauce in greased casserole dish. Mix butter and breadcrumbs, and top casserole with breadcrumbs. Bake in 350° oven for 20–30 minutes.
Yield: 8 servings

Green Rice

1 (8-ounce) package frozen chopped spinach
1½ cups cooked rice
2 tablespoons ground onion
¼ teaspoon granulated garlic salt
8 tablespoons margarine
2 cups milk
1 teaspoon salt
2 eggs
1¼ cups grated sharp Cheddar cheese

Cook spinach according to directions on package. Mix rice, onion, spinach, garlic salt, margarine, milk, and salt together. Beat eggs thoroughly. Add cheese and eggs to other ingredients. Put into large casserole dish and bake for 1 hour in 300° oven.
Yield: 12 servings

Sweet Potato Casserole

3 cups canned sweet potatoes
½ cup sugar
½ teaspoon salt
4 tablespoons margarine
½ cup milk
1½ teaspoons vanilla extract
2 eggs, beaten
about 2 cups Topping

Mix sweet potatoes, sugar, salt, margarine, milk, vanilla, and eggs. Spoon into 1½-quart baking dish. Crumble Topping over potatoes, if desired. Bake in 350° oven for 35 minutes.
Yield: 10 servings

Topping

½ cup brown sugar
⅓ cup all-purpose flour
1 cup chopped pecans
2⅔ tablespoons margarine

Mix well until smooth.
Yield: About 2 cups

Corn Pudding

4 eggs
1 tablespoon sugar
3 tablespoons all-purpose flour
3 cups whole-kernel corn
2 tablespoons margarine
½ teaspoon salt
dash of pepper
1½ cups milk, warm

Beat eggs thoroughly. Add sugar and flour together and add to egg mixture. Mix corn, margarine, salt, pepper, and warm milk together. Add to egg mixture. Pour into greased 1½-quart casserole dish. Bake in 300° oven for about 45 minutes.

Yield: 10 servings

Aunt Hattie's Squash Soufflé

1 cup breadcrumbs
½ cup powdered milk
4 cups boiled and drained squash; reserve broth
2 tablespoons ground onion powder
1 tablespoon ground green bell pepper
2 eggs
2 tablespoons sugar
1 teaspoon salt
2 tablespoons margarine, melted

Soak breadcrumbs and powdered milk in 2 cups squash broth for 15 minutes. Add to squash. Add onion and green pepper to mixture. Beat eggs well and add to squash mixture. Add sugar, salt, and margarine to ingredients and pour into greased 1½-quart casserole dish. Bake in 300° oven for 35 minutes.

Yield: 10 servings

Velda's Eggplant Casserole

1 medium eggplant
dash of salt
dash of pepper
1 tablespoon sugar
1 small onion
2 eggs
1 cup milk
4 tablespoons butter or margarine
½ cup breadcrumbs

Peel the eggplant, cut in chunks, and boil until tender, about 15 minutes. Drain well and mash. Add salt, pepper, and sugar. Finely chop onion and add to mixture. Beat eggs well and add milk. Add to eggplant mixture. Melt butter or margarine and mix with breadcrumbs. Top eggplant mixture with buttered breadcrumbs. Bake in 400° oven for 25 minutes.

Yield: 8 servings

Okra, Tomatoes, and Onions

1 (10-ounce) package frozen cut okra
1 large onion
3 cups canned tomatoes

Thaw okra. Slice onion in rings. Mix okra, onion slices, and tomatoes together. Cook slowly on low heat in heavy boiler for about 30 minutes or until onions and okra are thoroughly cooked.
Yield: 8 servings

The first time my mother heard the words *candy roaster* was shortly after we moved to these mountains, and she thought that it was the name of a black pot with legs. When our cook stopped laughing, she told my mother that the pot was called a spider pot, and a candy roaster was a bright orange (usually) fall squash. Nothing is better in the fall to serve with country ham and baked apples.

Candy Roaster

1 small candy roaster squash
½ cup brown sugar
¼ teaspoon cinnamon
salt to taste
¼ cup melted butter or margarine

Wash the candy roaster with a pot scrubber. Remove seeds and pulp, and cut into 3-inch squares. Drop squares into boiling water for about 3–5 minutes (or until fork barely sticks in pulp). Take out, drain very well, and place 12 pieces of 3-inch squares of candy roaster onto baking pan. Freeze the rest for use later. Make thick paste of brown sugar, cinnamon (add more to taste, if desired), salt to taste, and melted butter or margarine. Ice candy roaster with topping and bake in 375° oven for about 20 minutes or until topping bubbles. (Be careful not to cook too long as brown sugar is easily scorched.)
Yield: 12 pieces

Hemlock Train Wreck

2 cups or approximately
4 medium zucchini
2 large onions
1 teaspoon salt
½ teaspoon pepper
1 tablespoon dried basil
½ cup ketchup
¹/₃ cup real bacon bits

Wash but do not peel zucchini. Cut into slices. Slice onions and separate into rings. Slightly brown onions. In 1½-quart casserole dish place a layer of zucchini slices, and sprinkle with salt, pepper, and dried basil, and dot with ketchup. Cover with layer of onions and bacon bits. Repeat until casserole dish is filled. Cover with foil and cook in 350° oven for 1½ hours.
Yield: 10 servings

Hemlock Inn Broiled Tomatoes

4 large tomatoes
½ teaspoon salt
¹/₈ teaspoon pepper
1 cup breadcrumbs
1 cup Parmesan cheese
2 tablespoons melted butter

Cut tomatoes into thick slices. Sprinkle with salt and pepper. Add breadcrumbs to cover slices. Sprinkle with Parmesan cheese. Drizzle with melted butter. Broil until brown, about 5 minutes.
Yield: 12 servings

In high school, I, much like my boys, shared dining room responsibilities with many of my good friends. My dear friend Rita worked many summers both before and after me. One summer night while waiting to bring dinner to the table, she looked down at the zucchini casserole (round slices of zucchini dotted with ketchup) sitting on the warming table and said, "My word, Mrs. Shell! This looks like a train wreck!" And thus the dish was named Hemlock Train Wreck.

Summer Squash Casserole

6 cups sliced yellow summer squash
1 cup sliced onion
pinch of salt
1 (11.75-ounce) can condensed
cream of mushroom soup
1 cup sour cream
1 tablespoon lemon juice
1 (8-ounce) package herb-seasoned
stuffing crumbs
½ cup melted butter or margarine

Cook sliced squash and onion in salted boiling water for 5 minutes. Drain well in colander. Combine mushroom soup, sour cream, and lemon juice, and heat on low heat, about 10 minutes. Fold in squash and onion. Combine stuffing crumbs and butter. Spread half of stuffing mixture in bottom of 9-by-13-inch baking dish. Spoon vegetable mixture on top. Sprinkle remaining stuffing mixture over vegetables. Bake at 350° for 25–30 minutes.
Yield: 6 servings

Cream Cheese Mashed Potatoes

5 pounds potatoes, peeled and cut
1 (6-ounce) container cream cheese
1 (8-ounce) container sour cream
½ cup softened butter
½ cup milk
2 teaspoons onion salt
½ cup shredded Cheddar cheese,
optional

Cover potatoes with water in large saucepan and boil for 20 minutes. Drain and add all other ingredients except cheese. Beat on medium speed until fluffy, about 10 minutes. Grease 9-by-13-inch baking dish and pour potatoes into dish. Bake uncovered at 350° for 50 minutes. Sprinkle cheese on top, if desired.
Yield: 12 servings

Frosted Cauliflower

1 head cauliflower
½ cup mayonnaise
2 teaspoons prepared mustard
¾ cup shredded sharp Cheddar cheese

Cook cauliflower, leaving whole, in boiling water 10–15 minutes until tender. Drain and place whole cauliflower in shallow casserole dish. Frost with mayonnaise mixed with mustard. Sprinkle with cheese. Bake in 350° oven until cheese melts, about 10 minutes.
Yield: 8 servings

Eggplant Parmesan

2 large eggplants
2 cups breadcrumbs
½ teaspoon oregano
½ teaspoon garlic powder
½ teaspoon salt
¼ teaspoon pepper
4–6 cups Mil's Spaghetti Sauce
  (see page 73)
¼ cup grated Parmesan cheese
1 cup grated mozzarella cheese

Wash, drain, and peel eggplants. Slice into 1-inch pieces. Mix breadcrumbs, oregano, garlic powder, salt, and pepper together. Roll eggplant pieces in breadcrumb mixture. Place on oiled baking tray and put in 400° oven for about 20 minutes. In 9-by-13-inch casserole, pour a small amount of Mil's Spaghetti Sauce, just enough to cover bottom and to keep eggplant from sticking. Put pieces of eggplant over spaghetti sauce. Pour layer of spaghetti sauce on top of eggplant. Sprinkle half of Parmesan and mozzarella cheese on top of spaghetti sauce. Repeat eggplant, spaghetti sauce, and cheeses once more, ending with the cheeses as topping. Bake in 350° oven for 30–45 minutes or until bubbly and cheese is melted.

Yield: 10 servings

Note: Mil's Spaghetti Sauce has beef in it.

Alma's Stuffed Green Peppers

8 medium green bell peppers
6 tablespoons chopped onion
8 tablespoons margarine
1 pound ground beef
1 teaspoon poultry seasoning
1½ cups cooked white long-grain rice
½ teaspoon salt
¼ teaspoon pepper
1 (8-ounce) can tomato sauce

Wash peppers; cut in half from stem end. Remove seeds. Cover with boiling water (slightly salted), and boil uncovered 3–5 minutes. Drain. Brown onion in margarine, and add ground beef; cook for about 5 minutes. Add poultry seasoning, rice, salt, and pepper. Add tomato sauce to meat-and-rice mixture. Fill peppers with mixture and place in baking dish. Bake in 400° oven 15–20 minutes.

Yield: 12 servings

POULTRY

Our Heavenly Father, we do hunger and thirst after righteousness, and our prayer is that Thou would fill our hearts. We come now to receive Thy grace, and we thank Thee for Thy continued mercy. We thank Thee for a new day, for Thy strength, and now for this food. In Jesus' blessed name we ask it. Amen.

Annette's Chicken Salad

1 (4- or 5-pound) hen
3 stalks celery
1 teaspoon salt
¼ teaspoon pepper
12 pieces of white or light pickles
4 eggs, hard-boiled
1½ cups slivered almonds
2 cups white seedless grapes, halved
3 cups mayonnaise
12 slices pineapple
12 leaves of lettuce

Put hen in large pot and cover with salted water. (We use a 16-quart aluminum pot.) Bring to boil, cover, and turn heat down to low. Cook approximately 3 hours, or until chicken falls off the bone easily. Remove bones. Cut chicken into small pieces. Chop 2 cups celery (using only tender parts). Mix together with salt, pepper, pickles, eggs, almonds, grapes, and mayonnaise. Let stand in refrigerator about 1 hour. Serve on a slice of pineapple that has been placed on a crisp lettuce leaf.

Yield: 12 servings

Millie was a dear guest from Princeton, New Jersey.

Millie's Hot Chicken Salad

2 cups cooked and diced chicken
1 cup cream of chicken soup
1 cup diced celery
¼ teaspoon pepper
1 tablespoon lemon juice
¾ cup mayonnaise
2 teaspoons minced onions
½ cup chopped English walnuts
½ teaspoon salt
3 eggs, hard-boiled and thinly sliced
2 cups crushed potato chips
parsley

Combine all ingredients except potato chips and parsley. Pour into 8-by-12-inch pan. Top with crushed potato chips. Bake in 350° oven for 20 minutes. Garnish with parsley.

Yield: 8 servings

Chicken and Dumplings

2 (5-pound) baking hens
1 tablespoon salt
2 cups self-rising flour
¼ cup vegetable oil
1 egg
½ cup milk
2 tablespoons all-purpose flour
salt and pepper to taste
poultry seasoning, if desired

Put hens in large pot and cover with salted water. (We use a 16-quart aluminum pot.) Bring to boil, cover, and turn heat down to low. Cook approximately 3 hours, or until chicken falls off the bone easily. Remove hens from water, drain but reserve broth, remove all bones and skin, and set aside. Mix 2 cups flour, oil, egg, and milk together in mixing bowl until soft dough is formed. Turn out on board. Knead to rolling consistency. Roll out approximately ⅛-inch thick and cut into 3-inch strips. For thickening, gradually stir 2 tablespoons flour into broth from cooking chickens and bring to rolling boil. Add salt and pepper to taste. You may add poultry seasoning, but be careful not to make the broth too strong. Cut broth mixture down to simmer and drop 3-inch dumplings into pot. Cook approximately 10 minutes. Dip dumplings along with some of the thickened broth onto a deep platter. Place pieces of chicken around the outside of the platter.

Yield: 20 servings

Fried Chicken Batter

3 cups all-purpose flour
3 teaspoons paprika
4 teaspoons salt
1 teaspoon pepper

Mix ingredients together and put in paper bag. Shake damp chicken in bag. Use breasts, legs, or thighs. Place chicken in black skillet with ¼ inch vegetable oil. Cook at medium for 1 hour. The flour can be used several times if kept in air-tight container. Serve Fried Chicken with Chicken Gravy.

Chicken Gravy

3 tablespoons all-purpose flour
3 cups milk

Leave ¼ cup hot grease in black skillet after frying chicken. Add flour and stir constantly over medium heat until base begins to brown, about 5 minutes. Slowly add milk and stir with whisk until it thickens.

Yield: 2 cups

Chicken Pie

2 cups cooked and diced chicken
½ teaspoon salt
¹/₈ teaspoon pepper
3 tablespoons all-purpose flour
3 cups chicken broth
1 Piecrust (see page 142)

Put chicken in 8-by-12-inch glass baking dish. Mix salt, pepper, flour, and broth together. Pour broth over chicken. Cover with Piecrust and bake in 375° oven for 45 minutes or until crust is golden brown.

Yield: 10 servings

Note: We use chicken that has been frozen, or we use cooked chicken parts such as wings, backs, and pieces that we don't use for frying. If you don't have broth from a cooked chicken, you can make broth by using 1½ heaping tablespoons chicken soup base and 3 cups water.

Chicken Livers

Salt and pepper chicken livers, and put a small amount of flour on them. Cover with vegetable oil heated to 350° in deep fryer, and cook until well done, about 5 minutes. The livers must be done, but not crisp, and juicy, not dry. Remove from fryer and drain well on rack. Serve piping hot.

Note: Chicken livers must be of good quality and fresh. (They may be frozen but not old.)

E. J.'s Easy Chicken Tetrazzini

1 medium onion, chopped
2 tablespoons butter
¼ cup finely chopped green bell pepper
2 (10.75-ounce) cans cream of chicken soup (undiluted)
2 (10.75-ounce) cans cream of celery soup (undiluted)
2 cups white meat chicken, cooked
1 (2-ounce) jar chopped pimento
1 (4.5-ounce) jar sliced cooked mushrooms, drained
pinch of pepper
1 cup cooking sherry
1 (1-pound) box vermicelli

Sauté chopped onion in butter. Add pepper. Stir in chicken and celery soups and add cooked chicken. Add pimento and mushrooms. Sprinkle in pepper and pour in cooking sherry. Cook slowly for about 20 minutes at medium heat. Cook pasta according to directions and drain. Stir in chicken mixture.

Yield: 6 servings

This tetrazzini is great when made with Thanksgiving turkey leftovers instead of chicken.

Sister Jeanne's Chicken

1 teaspoon salt
¼ teaspoon pepper
8 boned chicken breast halves
1 (16-ounce) jar dried beef
4 slices bacon
1 (8-ounce) carton sour cream
1 (10.75-ounce) can cream of mushroom soup (undiluted)

Salt and pepper chicken breasts. Wrap 2 pieces of dried beef around chicken. Cut bacon in two halves. Wrap half slice bacon around chicken and hold together with toothpick. Mix sour cream and soup together. Spoon on top of chicken. Bake uncovered in 275° oven 2½–3 hours.

Yield: 8 servings

Jeanne was my father's sister.

PORK

Our Heavenly Father, we come to Thee in the
powerful and holy name of Jesus. We come lift-
ing our hands and hearts to Thee in praise. We are
so thankful Thou dost love us and care for us. We
thank Thee for this beautiful day and for Thy mercy,
for these friends and now for this food. In Jesus'
blessed name we ask it. Amen.

Pork Loin with Caramelized Onions

1 (2-pound) pork loin
1 teaspoon salt
½ teaspoon pepper
1 teaspoon seasoned salt
4 medium onions, sliced
⅛ cup sugar
2 tablespoons vegetable oil

Sprinkle the pork with salt, pepper, and seasoned salt. Place pork loin in roasting pan and cover or wrap in foil. Bake at 350° approximately 1 hour and 10 minutes. Meat thermometer should read 160°. Meanwhile, sauté onions with sugar in oil, about 10 minutes. Serve onions with pork loin.

Yield: 10 servings

Note: We use Lawry's seasoned salt.

Baked Ham

Rub ham with pepper. Place ham on roaster pan on rack. Cover and cook at 325°. Cook 30 minutes per pound.

My mom baked the best ham on earth! Her trick was to buy the butt portion, season with "lots" of pepper, and cook it slowly. We buy large "football" boneless hams from our wholesaler. Two 10-pound hams will feed 70 people on Thanksgiving Day.

Country Ham

Our country hams come from Clifty Farm in Tennessee. A small amount of oil is put in a black skillet and heated until a drop of water in the skillet bubbles. Slices of country ham are then placed in the skillet and cooked at medium heat only until slightly brown. Most people overcook good ham. It's already cured—you just want to make it tasty!

Red-Eye Gravy
¼ cup ham grease
2 cups strong black coffee

After you have fried your Country Ham, pour off excess grease and leave ¼ cup grease in black skillet. While still hot, pour in coffee and simmer 2–3 minutes.
Yield: 2 cups

Carolyn's Sausage Rice
½ cup white long-grain rice
1 (10-ounce) box chicken noodle soup
4½ cups chicken broth
2–3 stalks celery
¼ cup chopped onion
¼ cup chopped green bell pepper
2 tablespoons vegetable oil or margarine
1 pound bulk pork sausage
½ cup slivered almonds, if desired

Cook rice, chicken noodle soup, and broth for 7 minutes at medium heat. Sauté celery, onion, and bell pepper in oil or margarine, about 5 minutes, and add to soup mixture. Cook sausage at medium heat for 10 minutes; drain and crumble. Mix sausage with soup-and-rice mixture. Add almonds, if desired. Bake in 1½-quart casserole dish in 350° oven 1 hour.
Yield: 6–8 servings
Note: You may use canned chicken broth. This recipe freezes well.

Pork

Bacon

An often-asked question is, "How do you get your bacon so straight?" Daddy's answer was always, "We iron it." The truth is that we cook our bacon in a 350° oven stacked on racks that have been placed in a pan to collect the grease. Bacon is laid on cake-cooling racks that fit into a shallow baking pan. In cooking 1 pound of bacon, lay no more than nine pieces on each rack (do not let pieces touch). Stack racks one on top of the other. The drippings will have to be drained several times during cooking. It is taken out of the oven and wiped with a paper towel to remove excess grease. We buy only top-grade breakfast bacon.

E. J.'s Pork Chop Dish

4 (1-inch) center-cut pork chops
1 medium onion, sliced
1 medium green bell pepper, sliced
4 heaping teaspoons uncooked rice
1 teaspoon salt
$^1/_8$ teaspoon pepper
1 (16-ounce) can whole tomatoes

Put pork chops in 1½-quart casserole dish. Put slice of onion and slice of bell pepper on each pork chop. Place 1 heaping teaspoon of rice in middle of each pork chop. Sprinkle salt and pepper all over. Put ½ cup tomatoes on each pork chop. Cover dish with foil, and bake in 350° oven 1 hour.
Yield: 4 servings

This was one of my favorite dinners growing up.

Streak-o-lean

We buy the best of streak-o-lean, or fatback, or salt pork, or whatever you call it in your part of the country. It is sliced very thin and placed in sugar water the night before we serve it. We use only a small amount of sugar— approximately 1 teaspoon to 2 quarts of water. The morning of serving, the streak-o-lean is drained well, dipped in a small amount of flour, and fried very slowly in hot vegetable oil that barely covers the meat. The streak-o-lean is fried until it is golden crisp. It has been called Georgia Chicken, Sawmill Chicken, Tennessee Chicken, Bryson City T-Bone, and Country Bacon, or you may call it something else, but when we serve it with country gravy, it surely is popular!

To make the gravy, pour off all but about ½ cup grease. Stir in 2 tablespoons of flour, and stir constantly until brown. Slowly add about 1½–2 cups milk to flour mixture and stir constantly until it is as thick as desired. We do not add salt because grease will be pretty salty; you may add it if you want. The gravy makes about 1½–2 cups.

BEEF

Our Heavenly Father, we thank Thee for Thy
watchcare, and we thank Thee for Thy guidance.
We thank Thee for this lovely day, for good friends,
and Thy continued mercy. We are especially
thankful for times when we might wait on Thee.
We have felt Thy presence this day, and for this
we are so grateful. Thank you now for this food.
In Jesus' name we ask it. Amen.

Mary Ann's Steak

Marinade
6 tablespoons margarine, melted
1 tablespoon tenderizer
1 garlic clove, chopped
1 teaspoon salt
½ teaspoon cayenne pepper

Mix all ingredients together.
Yield: 4 servings

Steak
4 medium frozen steaks

Pour marinade over frozen steaks in
10-by-13-inch pan lined with foil.
Bake at 300° for 3½ hours,
or bake at 200° for 8 hours.
Yield: 4 servings

These steaks, with the warmth of the stove and the aroma drifting throughout the house, are quite tasty on a cold winter day. They go well with Cream Cheese Mashed Potatoes (see page 92).

Barbecued Beef Meatballs
1 pound ground beef
²/₃ teaspoon salt
1 tablespoon chopped onion
½ cup breadcrumbs
¼ cup milk
¼ cup all-purpose flour
2 tablespoons molasses
¼ cup white vinegar
¼ cup ketchup
¼ teaspoon hot sauce
¼ teaspoon oregano

Mix beef, salt, and onion together. Soak breadcrumbs in milk for 10 minutes. Add to beef mixture. Make meatballs and roll in small amount of flour. Place meatballs in a saucepan and brown quickly but do not cook completely. In separate dish, combine molasses, vinegar, ketchup, hot sauce, and oregano; mix well. Cover meatballs with sauce. Cook in oven for 20 minutes at 350°.
Yield: approximately 14 small balls
Note: We use Tabasco hot sauce.

Country Fried Steak

1 teaspoon salt
$^1/_8$ teaspoon pepper
½ cup all-purpose flour
½ cup vegetable oil
1½ pounds round cubed steak

Mix salt, pepper, and flour together. Have oil hot. Dip steak into flour mixture and brown well on both sides in black skillet 2 minutes on each side. Remove from heat and place steak in roaster pan with rack in bottom to keep from sticking. Pour leftover flour mixture into black skillet, brown, and add water to make gravy. Gravy ratio is 1 tablespoon flour, ¼ teaspoon salt, and a pinch of pepper to 1 cup water. Make as much gravy as needed to slightly cover steak. Place covered roaster pan in 375° oven for 1½ hours.

Yield: 6 servings

Note: The secret of all good meat is to buy only prime or choice meat. And be sure you have a dependable meat market.

Blue Cheese Turnovers

2 medium onions, chopped
2 tablespoons bacon fat or olive oil
1 pound lean ground beef
½ cup breadcrumbs
½ teaspoon dry mustard
¼ teaspoon garlic salt
¼ teaspoon basil
¼ teaspoon paprika
1 tablespoon Worcestershire sauce
½ cup crumbled blue cheese
1 Piecrust (see page 142)

Slightly brown onions in oil. Add beef to onions and brown. Add crumbs, mustard, garlic salt, basil, paprika, and Worcestershire sauce to meat mixture and cook about 10 minutes on low heat. Cool.

Add blue cheese to mixture and mix well. Meanwhile, cut Piecrust into 4-inch squares. Put tablespoon of mixture into 4-inch pastry squares, fold, and seal, like an apple tart. Bake in 375° oven for 15 minutes or until brown.

Yield: 24 servings

Note: This was one of Mrs. Haynie's specialties.

Beef Pie

2 cups minced roast beef
½ teaspoon salt
¹/₈ teaspoon pepper
3 tablespoons all-purpose flour
3 cups beef broth
1 Piecrust (see page 142)

Cut beef in bite-size pieces. Put beef in shallow 8-by-10-inch glass baking dish. Mix salt, pepper, flour, and broth together. Pour broth over beef. Cover with Piecrust and bake in 375° oven for 45 minutes or until crust is golden brown.

Yield: 10 servings

Note: We use leftover beef from our beef roasts. We use only choice or prime beef, so be sure pieces of beef are tender. If you don't have broth from your beef roast, you can make broth by using 2 heaping tablespoons beef soup base and 3 cups water.

Corned Beef Hash

2 pounds potatoes
¾ cup ground onions
2 cups cooked corned beef
2 slightly rounded tablespoons beef bouillon

Finely grate potatoes and mix with onions and corned beef. Mix beef bouillon with 1⅓ cups hot water and pour over mixture. Place in covered roaster pan in 350° oven for about 1 hour or until potatoes are done. When ready to serve, warm in casserole dish and serve hot.

Yield: 12 servings

Hemlock Inn Meat Loaf

3 pounds ground beef
½ cup ketchup
1 cup chopped onions
6 eggs
1 teaspoon salt
1 tablespoon Worcestershire sauce
²/₃ cup breadcrumbs
²/₃ cup stewed tomatoes
4 tablespoons butter (optional)

Mix all ingredients together well and put in greased 1½-quart loaf pan. Bake in 350° oven for 1 hour.

Yield: 20 servings

Corn Bread Meat Loaf

1 pound ground beef
½ pound ground bulk pork sausage
1 egg
1 cup corn bread crumbs
1 medium onion, chopped
1½ teaspoons salt
¼ teaspoon pepper
1 cup tomato sauce, divided
2 tablespoons white vinegar
2 tablespoons prepared mustard
2 tablespoons brown sugar

Mix ground beef, sausage, egg, corn bread crumbs, onion, salt, pepper, and ½ cup tomato sauce. Mold into mound and put in greased 1½-quart loaf pan. Combine 1 cup water, vinegar, ½ cup tomato sauce, mustard, and brown sugar. Pour half of sauce over meat loaf. Bake in 325° oven for about 45 minutes. With remaining sauce, baste several times while baking.
Yield: 6 servings

Eye of Round

Have eye of round roast at room temperature. Preheat oven to 500°. Sprinkle with coarse black pepper or other seasoning. Place round in a roaster and cover. Bake 5 minutes per pound. Turn off and do not open oven for 2 hours. Roast will be pink.

SEAFOOD

Our Heavenly Father, we would truly come to Thee as this new day starts and pray that Thou would somehow draw us close to Thee and lift us to a loftier level. We thank Thee for Thy strength, and now for this food. In Jesus' name we ask it. Amen.

Easy Tuna Casserole

½ cup mayonnaise
¼ cup minced onion
1 teaspoon salt
1 cup cream of celery soup
½ cup milk
½ cup grated sharp Cheddar cheese
1 (8-ounce) package macaroni noodles
1 (7-ounce) can solid pack white tuna fish

Heat together mayonnaise, onion, salt, soup, milk, and cheese on low heat until cheese melts. Cook noodles according to package directions, drain, and place in 1½-quart baking dish. Add tuna to heated sauce mixture. Pour mixture over noodles. Bake in 425° oven 20 minutes.
Yield: 8 servings

Mary's Tuna Bake

1 (8-ounce) can white flaked tuna
1 (10-ounce) can cream of mushroom soup
1 (2-ounce) package potato chips

Drain tuna well and mix together with soup. Crush potato chips and mix in tuna mixture. Put in 1½-quart baking dish and bake in 350° oven about 30 minutes.
Yield: 4 servings

Mildred's Baked Fish

½ cup mayonnaise
¼ cup prepared mustard
juice of ½ lemon
½ teaspoon salt
¼ teaspoon paprika
¼ teaspoon garlic salt
1 (1-pound) package frozen cod fillets

Mix together mayonnaise, mustard, lemon juice, salt, paprika, and garlic salt. Cut codfish into 2-inch squares and put in greased 1½-quart casserole dish. Pour mayonnaise mixture over fish. Bake in 350° oven 30–45 minutes.
Yield: 8 servings

Note: In our kitchen, we partially thaw frozen packages of codfish. Do not separate fish, but cut into 2-inch squares the depth of the frozen codfish package.

Shrimp and Grits

Our shrimp and grits recipe is in three parts: the shrimp, the rosemary-tomato sauce, and the grits. Together they form a Southern delicacy.

Shrimp

1 pound large shrimp
2 tablespoons Cajun seasoning

Peel shrimp. Starting at tail end, butterfly each shrimp, cutting to, but not through, top of shrimp. Heat a nonstick skillet coated with cooking spray over medium heat. Add shrimp and seasoning; sauté 3 minutes or until shrimp are done.

Grits

2 cups water
¼ teaspoon salt
¼ teaspoon garlic powder
⅛ teaspoon dry mustard
¹/₈ teaspoon paprika
½ cup uncooked grits
¼ cup (1 ounce) shredded sharp Cheddar cheese
2 teaspoons butter or margarine

Bring first 5 ingredients to a boil. Stir in grits; cover, reduce heat, and simmer 20 minutes, stirring occasionally. Stir in cheese and butter. Spoon grits onto plate; top with shrimp. Spoon Rosemary-Tomato Sauce evenly around shrimp.

Yield: 4 servings

Rosemary-Tomato Sauce

2 teaspoons olive oil
1 cup diced onion
1½ cups diced red bell pepper
1 tablespoon chopped fresh rosemary or 1 teaspoon dried rosemary
4 cups coarsely chopped peeled tomato
½ cup dry white wine
¼ teaspoon salt
8 garlic cloves, minced

Heat oil in a large saucepan over medium-high heat. Add onion; sauté 3 minutes. Add bell pepper and rosemary; sauté 1 minute. Stir in tomato, wine, salt, and garlic; bring to a boil. Reduce heat and simmer 30 minutes.

Cornelia's Tuna Salad

1 (8-ounce) can solid pack white tuna
1 cup chopped celery
2 cups grated carrots
2 small onions, chopped
1 cup mayonnaise
1 cup chopped stuffed olives
3 eggs, hard-boiled
1 cup chopped cashews
1 cup chow mein noodles

Mix tuna, celery, carrots, onions, mayonnaise, olives, and eggs together and put in refrigerator until ready to serve. Mixture will keep for 24 hours in refrigerator. Toss cashews and noodles into the tuna mixture just before serving.
Yield: 8 servings

Pat's Tuna Bake

1 egg
½ cup uncooked instant rice
1½ cups grated sharp Cheddar cheese, divided
1 (14-ounce) can solid pack white tuna, drained
½ cup sliced stuffed olives
2 tablespoons parsley
1 tablespoon instant minced onion
2 teaspoons dry mustard
1 teaspoon salt
dash of pepper
1 (13-ounce) can evaporated milk

In ungreased 2-quart casserole dish, beat egg slightly. Mix in rice, 1⅛ cups of cheese, tuna, olives, and seasonings. Stir in milk and ½ cup water. Sprinkle remaining cheese on top. Cover and bake in 350° oven for 40 minutes.
Yield: 10 servings

Thelma's Tuna Macaroni Casserole

1 cup uncooked macaroni
1 heaping tablespoon finely chopped onion
2 tablespoons margarine
¼ cup all-purpose flour
1¼ cups milk
¼ teaspoon salt
1 teaspoon Worcestershire sauce
1 heaping teaspoon prepared mustard
1 cup grated sharp Cheddar cheese
1 (7-ounce) can solid pack white tuna
½ cup breadcrumbs, if desired
2 tablespoons butter, if desired
⅛ teaspoon paprika, if desired

Cook macaroni according to package directions, drain, and let set in cold water for 10 minutes. Sauté onions slightly, until tender. Combine margarine, flour, milk, and salt, and cook on low heat until thick, about 5 minutes. Add Worcestershire sauce, mustard, and chopped onion to sauce. Add cheese to sauce mixture and stir until blended. Break up tuna and add to sauce. Mix drained macaroni with rest of ingredients, put in 1½-quart casserole dish, and bake in 325° oven 45 minutes. If desired, sprinkle top with breadcrumbs, dot with butter, and add paprika for garnish.
Yield: 8 servings

Salmon Patties with Pea Sauce

3 (15-ounce) cans salmon
3 medium eggs
⅛ cup diced red bell pepper
⅛ cup diced green bell pepper
⅛ cup diced onion
4 ounces saltine crackers, crushed
8 cups vegetable oil
½ cup peas (fresh, frozen, or canned)
1 cup White Sauce

Mix first 6 ingredients together. Mold into 4-inch patties. Deep-fry on medium heat in oil 5 minutes on each side. Stir peas into White Sauce, and pour on top of patties.
Yield: 25 patties

White Sauce

1 tablespoon butter
1 tablespoon all-purpose flour
pinch of salt
1 cup milk

In heavy saucepan, melt butter. Stir in flour and salt, and slowly add milk. Stir constantly with whisk until thick.
Yield: 1 cup

> # Bobbye was another Girl Scout leader of mine.

Bobbye's Shrimp and Chicken Creole

1 medium onion
½ cup chopped green bell pepper
3 garlic cloves
1½ cups cooked rice
4 tablespoons butter or margarine
1 (16-ounce) can tomatoes (whole or diced)
1 teaspoon salt
dash of cayenne pepper
2 (5- or 6-ounce) cans boned chicken
2 (4- or 5-ounce) cans shrimp
¾ cup grated sharp Cheddar cheese
¼ pound sliced sharp Cheddar cheese

Grate onion and sauté with bell pepper, garlic, and rice in butter or margarine for 3–5 minutes. Remove from heat. Add tomatoes, salt, and cayenne pepper. Mix well. Cut chicken in bite-size pieces and add liquid from chicken. Drain shrimp and add. Put half of mixture in 9-by-13-inch casserole dish and sprinkle grated cheese over it. Add rest of mixture. Cover and bake in preheated 350° oven 20–25 minutes. Remove from oven and arrange 1-inch-wide strips of cheese over top and return to oven 2–3 minutes to melt slightly.
Yield: 8 servings

Barbara's Salmon Loaf

1 (16-ounce) can salmon
1 (10.75-ounce) can cream of celery soup
1 cup breadcrumbs
2 eggs
½ cup chopped onions
1 tablespoon lemon juice

Mix all ingredients together well.
Grease 1½-quart loaf pan and line with
wax paper. Pour ingredients in pan.
Bake in 375° oven for 1 hour.
Cool 10 minutes. Turn out and serve.
Yield: 8 servings

Pecan-Crusted Baked Trout

8 (6-ounce) trout fillets
1 tablespoon crushed rosemary leaves
1 teaspoon salt
1 teaspoon crushed tarragon leaves
1 teaspoon pepper
2 cups breadcrumbs
1 cup chopped toasted pecans
½ cup margarine, melted

Place trout fillets in large baking pan,
skin side down. Mix remaining
ingredients together. Spoon mixture
on top of fillets, pressing the mixture
down on each fillet. Bake at 350° for
20 minutes in preheated oven.
Yield: 8 servings

Seafood Salad

1 (3-ounce) package lemon gelatin
½ cup chili sauce
1 tablespoon apple cider vinegar
3 drops hot sauce
1 teaspoon Worcestershire sauce
2 tablespoons horseradish
1 cup chopped celery
1 cup chopped green bell pepper
pinch of salt
1 cup canned or cooked shrimp
1 cup canned or cooked crab claw meat

Dissolve gelatin in 1 cup boiling
water. Mix chili sauce, vinegar,
hot sauce, Worcestershire, and
horseradish together in measuring
cup. Add cold water to ingredients
to make 1 cup of liquid. Add
gelatin mixture. Let set until
it starts to set, about 30 minutes.
Add celery, bell pepper, salt, and
seafood. Let gel, about 2 hours.
Refrigerate before serving.
Yield: 8 servings
*Note: This recipe is wonderful
for a luncheon.*

CAKES &
FROSTINGS

Our Heavenly Father, again how happy we are to truly come to Thee, and we come because of our needs and not because of our pride. We thank You for this lovely day and Thy continued mercy. We know that You love us because You suffer with us. Thank You now for these friends and this food. In Jesus' name we ask it. Amen.

Miss Betty's Cherry Cake Cobbler

8 tablespoons margarine
1¾ cups sugar, divided
1 cup all-purpose flour
2 teaspoons baking powder
¾ cup milk
1 (16-ounce) can pie cherries
½ teaspoon almond extract

Melt margarine in cobbler pan. Mix ¾ cup sugar, flour, baking powder, and milk together. Pour into melted margarine. Stir. Mix 1 cup sugar with cherries (undrained) and almond extract and bring to boil. Pour over batter mixture. Distribute cherries evenly with spoon. Bake in 350° oven for about 45 minutes.
Yield: 8 servings

Ruby D's Cake

1 (21-ounce) can cherry pie filling
1 (20-ounce) can crushed pineapple
1 (15.25-ounce) box yellow cake mix
16 tablespoons margarine, melted
1 (6-ounce) can coconut
1 cup chopped pecans

In bottom of 9-by-13-inch glass baking dish, place pie filling and pineapple (undrained). Sprinkle with cake mix. Pour melted margarine over cake mix. Top with coconut and pecans. Bake at 350° for approximately 1 hour.
Yield: 10–12 servings

Myrtle's Butternut Pound Cake

½ cup shortening
16 tablespoons butter
3 cups sugar
5 eggs
3 cups sifted all-purpose flour
½ teaspoon baking powder
¼ teaspoon salt
1 cup milk
1 tablespoon butternut flavoring

Blend shortening, butter, and sugar until creamy. Add eggs one at a time, beating after each one is added. Sift flour, baking powder, and salt together and add to shortening mixture alternately with milk. Add butternut flavoring. Pour in greased 9-inch tube pan and bake in 350° oven for 1 hour and 15 minutes.
Yield: 10–12 servings

Ruby DeHart was a local friend of my mother's.

E.J.'s Christmas Cake
1 large angel food cake
4 cups peppermint ice cream
2 cups whipped topping
½ cup crushed peppermint stick

Slice angel food cake into three layers.
Put bottom layer on a cake plate.
Put about 2 inches of peppermint ice
cream on top of cake, and cover with
second layer of cake. Put another
2 inches of ice cream, and put on top
layer of cake. Ice cake with whipped
topping. Sprinkle crushed peppermint
stick on top. Freeze overnight.
Cut and serve as desired.
Yield: 16 servings
*Note: This is also good with
chocolate ice cream.*

Banana Split Cake
1 (20-ounce) can crushed pineapple
8 tablespoons margarine
2 cups graham cracker crumbs
1 (8-ounce) package cream cheese
1 cup sugar
1 (9-ounce) container whipped topping
4–5 medium bananas
1 (6-ounce) jar Maraschino cherries
1 (5-ounce) jar wet walnuts

Drain pineapple (should drain about
2 hours). Melt margarine. Stir graham
cracker crumbs into melted margarine
and pack in 11-by-13-inch pan. Blend
together cream cheese, sugar, and
whipped topping. Slice bananas over
graham cracker crust to form the first
layer. Add one layer each of cheese mix,
bananas, and pineapple. Put cherries
and nuts on top layer. Chill until firm,
about 1 hour.
Yield: 12 servings

> # Mom always served this at Christmas parties.

Honey Bun Cake
1 (15.25-ounce) box yellow cake mix
4 eggs
¾ cup vegetable oil
¾ cup sour cream
1 cup brown sugar
1 tablespoon ground cinnamon
2 cups Honey Bun Glaze

Mix first 4 ingredients together.
Pour two-thirds of the batter into the
bottom of a greased 9-by-13-inch pan.
Sprinkle brown sugar and cinnamon
over first layer of batter. Top with
remaining batter. Bake at 325° for
45 minutes. Frost cake with Honey
Bun Glaze while still warm.
Yield: 10–12 servings

Honey Bun Glaze
2 cups confectioners' sugar
4–6 tablespoons milk

Add milk to sugar 1 tablespoon at a
time until the mixture is smooth.
Yield: 2 cups

Mil's Soft Gingerbread Cake

12 tablespoons butter
1½ cups sugar
1½ cups molasses
3 eggs, well beaten
4½ cups sifted all-purpose flour
3 tablespoons baking soda
3 tablespoons ground ginger
1 tablespoon ground cinnamon
1 teaspoon ground allspice
¾ teaspoon ground cloves
¾ teaspoon ground nutmeg
1½ cups buttermilk
4 cups Orange Sauce

Cream butter and sugar. Add molasses and eggs. Mix together other dry ingredients and add buttermilk. Mix well until no lumps. Pour into greased 9-by-13-inch pan and bake in 350° oven for 30–35 minutes. Pour Orange Sauce over cake, and serve warm.
Yield: 24 servings

Orange Sauce

1½ cups sugar
3 tablespoons cornstarch
½ teaspoon salt
1½ cups pulp-free orange juice
$^1/_3$ cup lemon juice
2 egg yolks
1½ tablespoons grated orange rind

Mix sugar, cornstarch, salt, and orange juice together. Add lemon juice and ⅓ cup water. Beat egg yolks and add to other ingredients. Stir in orange rind.
Yield: 4 cups

Mother's (Dody's) Chocolate Cake

2 cups all-purpose flour
2 cups sugar
1 cup vegetable oil
8 tablespoons butter
4 tablespoons unsweetened cocoa powder
½ cup buttermilk
2 eggs
½ teaspoon baking soda
pinch of salt
¾ cup Chocolate Icing

Combine flour and sugar in mixing bowl. Put 1 cup water, oil, butter, and cocoa into heavy boiler. Bring to a boil and cook 1 minute, stirring constantly. Add mixture to sugar and flour and beat well. Add buttermilk, eggs, baking soda, and salt. Mix until smooth. Pour batter in 9-by-13-inch pan and bake in 350° oven for 40 minutes. Ice with Chocolate Icing while still hot.
Yield: 18 servings

Chocolate Icing

4 tablespoons milk
4 tablespoons unsweetened cocoa powder
8 tablespoons butter
2 cups confectioners' sugar
1 teaspoon vanilla extract

Mix milk, cocoa, and butter together and bring to boil. Add confectioners' sugar and vanilla, stirring until well mixed, with no lumps.
Yield: ¾ cup

German Chocolate Pound Cake

1 (4-ounce) bar sweet German chocolate
2 cups sugar
1 cup shortening
4 eggs, well beaten
2 teaspoons vanilla extract
2 teaspoons butter flavoring
1 cup buttermilk
3 cups all-purpose flour
½ teaspoon baking soda
1 teaspoon salt
¾ cup Sweet Chocolate Cake Glaze

Partially melt chocolate over hot water in double boiler. Remove and stir rapidly until melted. Cool. Cream sugar and shortening. Add eggs, vanilla, butter flavoring, and buttermilk. Sift together flour, baking soda, and salt. Add to shortening mixture and mix well. Blend in chocolate. Pour into well-greased and floured 9-inch tube pan. Bake in 300° oven for about 1½ hours. Remove from pan while still hot and place under tightly fitted cover until thoroughly cooled. Ice with Sweet Chocolate Cake Glaze.
Yield: 18 servings

Sweet Chocolate Cake Glaze

1 (4-ounce) bar sweet German chocolate
1 tablespoon butter
1 cup sifted confectioners' sugar
dash of salt
½ teaspoon vanilla extract

Melt chocolate and butter in ¼ cup water over low heat. Mix in sugar and salt. Blend together and add vanilla. For thinner glaze, add a small amount of hot water.
Yield: ¾ cup

Hemlock Inn Birthday Cake

1 cup shortening
2 cups sugar
4 eggs
3 cups all-purpose flour
¾ teaspoon salt
1 teaspoon baking powder
1 cup milk
1 teaspoon vanilla extract

Cream shortening and add sugar. Add eggs one at a time. Sift flour, salt, and baking powder. Add flour mixture alternately with milk to shortening mixture. Fill 4 greased 1-pound coffee cans (or 4 loaf pans) half full. Bake in 350° oven for 1 hour.
Yield: 4 small cakes

Chocolate Pound Cake

16 tablespoons margarine
½ cup shortening
3 cups sugar
5 eggs
3 cups all-purpose flour
¼ teaspoon salt
½ teaspoon baking powder
½ cup unsweetened cocoa powder
1¼ cups milk
1 teaspoon vanilla extract

Cream margarine, shortening, and sugar together well. Add eggs one at a time, blending well after each. Sift together flour, salt, baking powder, and cocoa. Add to shortening mixture alternately with milk. Add vanilla. Pour into greased and floured 9-inch tube pan and bake in 325° oven for 1 hour and 25 minutes.
Yield: 18 servings

Raw Apple Cake

2 cups sugar
16 tablespoons margarine
4 eggs, beaten
½ teaspoon salt
3 cups all-purpose flour
2 teaspoons ground cinnamon
1 teaspoon ground mace
2 teaspoons baking soda
1 cup cold coffee
3 cups chopped apples
1 cup raisins
1 cup chopped pecans
2 tablespoons confectioners' sugar

Cream sugar and margarine.
Add eggs. Sift salt, flour, cinnamon,
mace, and baking soda. Add to sugar
mixture alternately with coffee.
Add apples, raisins, and nuts.
Bake in 9-inch tube pan in 350°
oven for 1 hour or until firm.
Sprinkle with confectioners' sugar.
Yield: 18 servings
Note: Any kind of apple is fine to use.
We use Granny Smith apples for cooking.

Spice Cake

1 cup quick oatmeal
½ cup shortening
1 cup brown sugar
1 cup sugar
2 eggs
1⅓ cups all-purpose flour
1 teaspoon baking soda
½ teaspoon salt
½ teaspoon ground cinnamon
½ teaspoon ground nutmeg
1 teaspoon vanilla extract
¾ cup Spice Cake Topping

Pour 1¼ cups boiling water over
oatmeal. Let stand 10 minutes. Cream
shortening, brown sugar, and sugar.
Add to oatmeal mixture. Add eggs one
at a time. Sift flour, baking soda, salt,
cinnamon, and nutmeg, and add to
mixture. Stir just enough to mix. Add
vanilla. Pour into greased 9-by-13-inch
pan and bake in 325° oven for 35–40
minutes. Spread Spice Cake Topping
on cake. Brown under low broiler,
about 8 minutes. Serve warm.
Yield: 18 servings

Spice Cake Topping

8 tablespoons margarine
1 cup brown sugar
2 egg yolks
1 cup well-drained crushed pineapple,
  if desired
1 cup chopped pecans, if desired

Cream margarine, sugar, and egg yolks
together. Add pineapple and nuts if
desired (we use one or the other).
Yield: ¾ cup

Pat's Carrot Cake

1½ cups all-purpose flour
1 cup sugar
1 teaspoon baking powder
1 teaspoon baking soda
1 teaspoon ground cinnamon
1½ teaspoons salt
²/₃ cup vegetable oil
2 eggs
1 cup finely shredded carrots
½ cup crushed pineapple with syrup
1 teaspoon vanilla extract
¾ cup Carrot Cake Icing

Mix first 6 ingredients together. Add oil, eggs, carrots, crushed pineapple, and vanilla. Beat 2 minutes at medium speed on electric mixer. Bake in greased and lightly floured 9-by-9-inch pan in 350° oven about 35 minutes. Cool completely, and spread on Carrot Cake Icing.
Yield: 12 servings

Carrot Cake Icing

1 (3-ounce) package cream cheese, softened
1 tablespoon softened butter
1 teaspoon vanilla extract
2 cups confectioners' sugar

With electric mixer on medium, beat all ingredients together until light and fluffy. If necessary, add milk to make spreading easier.
Yield: ¾ cup

> Easy Pound Cake was the first recipe my daughter-in-law asked for.

Rotten Coconut Cake

2 (15.25-ounce) boxes white cake mix
1 (21-ounce) can cream of coconut
1 (14-ounce) can sweetened condensed milk
1½ cups whipped topping
1 (6-ounce) can coconut

Bake cake as directed on box in one 9-by-13-inch pan. When cake is done, punch holes in cake with fork. Mix cream of coconut and condensed milk together and pour over hot cake. Let cool. Top with whipped topping and coconut.
Yield: 18 servings

Easy Pound Cake

16 tablespoons margarine
3 cups sugar
½ cup shortening
5 large eggs
3 cups all-purpose flour
½ teaspoon baking powder
¼ teaspoon salt
1 cup milk
4 teaspoons vanilla extract

Beat first 4 ingredients together until creamy. Sift flour, baking powder, and salt together. Add flour mixture and milk to wet ingredients alternately, ending with flour mixture. Add vanilla and mix. Bake 1½ hours at 325° in greased and floured Bundt pan.
Yield: 18 servings
Note: You may use more vanilla extract if you wish.

Dot's Prune Cake

1½ cups sugar
1 cup vegetable oil
3 eggs
2 cups all-purpose flour
1 teaspoon baking soda
½ teaspoon salt
1 teaspoon ground cinnamon
1 teaspoon ground nutmeg
1 teaspoon ground allspice
1 cup buttermilk
1 cup cooked and cut prunes
1 cup chopped pecans
1 teaspoon vanilla extract
¾ cup Prune Cake Icing

Mix sugar and oil together. Add eggs. Sift together flour, baking soda, salt, cinnamon, nutmeg, and allspice; add to sugar mixture alternately with buttermilk. Add prunes, nuts, and vanilla. Pour into buttered 9-inch tube pan or 9-by-12-inch sheet cake pan. Bake in 350° oven for 45 minutes (or until brown). Remove from oven. Pour icing over cake while still hot; it will soak into cake.
Yield: 18 servings

Prune Cake Icing

1 cup sugar
½ cup buttermilk
½ teaspoon baking soda
1 teaspoon light corn syrup
4 tablespoons butter
½ teaspoon vanilla extract

Mix all ingredients together in heavy saucepan and boil until drop in cold water forms ball, about 5 minutes.
Yield: ¾ cup

Sweet Potato Surprise Cake

1½ cups vegetable oil
2 cups sugar
4 eggs, separated
2½ cups sifted all-purpose flour
3 teaspoons baking powder
¼ teaspoon salt
1 teaspoon ground cinnamon
1 teaspoon ground nutmeg
1½ cups grated sweet potatoes
1 cup chopped pecans
1 teaspoon vanilla extract
1 cup Sweet Potato Cake Frosting

Combine oil and sugar and beat well until smooth. Add egg yolks and beat. Add 3 tablespoons hot water and flour, baking powder, salt, cinnamon, and nutmeg, which have been sifted together. Stir in sweet potatoes, nuts, and vanilla. Beat well 1–2 minutes until smooth. Beat egg whites until stiff and fold into mixture. Bake in greased 9-by-13-inch pan in 350° oven for 25–30 minutes. Cool and frost.
Yield: 12 servings

Sweet Potato Cake Frosting

1 (14.25-ounce) can evaporated milk
1 cup sugar
8 tablespoons margarine
3 egg yolks
1 teaspoon vanilla extract
1¹/₃ cups flaked coconut

Combine milk, sugar, margarine, egg yolks, and vanilla in heavy boiler and cook about 12 minutes until thick, stirring constantly. Remove from heat and add coconut. Beat until cool.
Yield: 1 cup

CANDIES &
COOKIES

Our dear Heavenly Father, Thou dost put a song in
our heart and we pause now to sing Thy praise. We
come simply to lift our hands and hearts to Thee in
worship and give thanks for this lovely day and for Thy
mercy. We are so thankful that Thou dost continue to
struggle with us. Thank You now for these friends and
for this food. In Jesus' name we ask it. Amen.

Simply Fudge

1²/₃ cups sugar
²/₃ cup evaporated milk
2 tablespoons butter
2 cups miniature marshmallows
1½ cups semisweet chocolate chips
2 teaspoons vanilla extract

Bring first 3 ingredients to a boil in a large heavy saucepan over medium heat. Boil, stirring constantly, until a candy thermometer registers 234° (about 7 minutes). Remove from heat; stir in marshmallows and chocolate chips until smooth. Stir in vanilla. Pour into a buttered 8-by-8-inch pan and cool completely in refrigerator, about 1 hour. Cut into 1-inch squares.

Yield: 64 pieces

Mama's Christmas Fudge

3 cups semisweet chocolate chips
3 (1.55-ounce) almond chocolate bars
2 cups marshmallow cream
4 tablespoons butter
4 cups chopped nuts (at least
   half almonds)
1²/₃ cups undiluted evaporated milk
4½ cups sugar

Put chocolate chips, almond chocolate bars, marshmallow cream, butter, and nuts in large mixing bowl. Combine milk and sugar in saucepan; boil for 5 minutes or until a candy thermometer reads 225°. Stir mixture constantly to keep from sticking. Remove from heat and pour over ingredients in mixing bowl. Stir with wooden spoon until chocolate is smooth. Spread on greased surface and cool, about 1–2 hours. Cut in squares when cool.

Yield: 48–60 squares

Mama refers to my mother, Ella Jo. This is another Christmas staple for our family Christmas.

Ice Box Cookies

1 cup sugar
1 cup brown sugar
¾ cup melted margarine or butter
¾ cup melted shortening
2 eggs, slightly beaten
4 cups self-rising flour
1 teaspoon vanilla extract

Mix sugars with melted margarine and shortening. Add eggs. Sift in flour and add vanilla. Mold in about 12-inch rolls, wrap in wax paper, and put in refrigerator or freezer or bake immediately. Slice dough just before baking. The dough will keep for a few weeks in the refrigerator. Bake in 350° oven for 10–12 minutes.

Yield: 60 cookies

Note: These can be found in the Hemlock Inn box lunches.

Betty Cass's Brown Sugar Cookies

½ cup shortening
2 cups brown sugar
2 eggs
2¼ cups self-rising flour
2 teaspoons vanilla extract
1 cup chopped pecans (or your choice)
8 tablespoons margarine

+ marg.

Cream shortening, and add sugar and eggs. Sift in flour and add vanilla and nuts. Mix well. Drop by teaspoons on buttered pan. Bake at 350° for 15 minutes.

Yield: 36 cookies

Refrigerator Cookies

16 tablespoons margarine
1 cup sugar
1 cup brown sugar
2 eggs
½ tablespoon butter flavoring
½ tablespoon brandy or rum
1 teaspoon baking soda
1 teaspoon salt
3½ cups all-purpose flour
1 cup chopped black walnuts

Cream margarine and sugars together. Fold in eggs. Add butter flavoring and brandy or rum. Sift baking soda, salt, and flour and stir enough flour mixture into sugar mixture for soft dough. Add chopped walnuts. Roll into long rolls 2 inches in diameter.
Wrap and refrigerate for a few days. Then slice and bake in 350° oven for 10–12 minutes. Dough can keep in refrigerator for up to 2 months.

Yield: 48 cookies

My sweet Dody (my mother's mother) passed away in 2005. When I last visited her at her nursing home in Tennessee, her Sunday school class brought her a Christmas gift—a box of this candy! It made me cry.

134

Dody's Peanut Butter Candy

4 tablespoons butter, softened
1/3 cup light corn syrup
1 teaspoon vanilla extract
1 (16-ounce) box confectioners' sugar
1/2 cup peanut butter

With fork, mix together butter, corn syrup, and vanilla. Gradually knead in sugar. When the mixture glistens, about 2 minutes, roll it out as thinly as possible on wax paper. Spread a thin layer of peanut butter on top. Roll the dough as tightly as possible in a jelly roll fashion. Cut into 1-inch pieces and refrigerate about an hour. Candy can keep up to 2 weeks in refrigerator.
Yield: 48 pieces

Molasses Cookies

1 egg
1 cup brown sugar
1 cup molasses
3/4 cup melted butter
1/8 teaspoon salt
1/4 cup all-purpose flour

Slightly beat egg, and add sugar, molasses, butter, 1/4 cup boiling water, and salt. Add just enough flour to knead. Roll dough, and cut out with your favorite cookie cutter. Bake in 400° oven for 8–10 minutes.
Yield: 24 cookies

Butterscotch Oatmeal Cookies

16 tablespoons margarine
2 cups brown sugar
2 eggs
2 teaspoons vanilla extract
1 teaspoon butter flavoring
4 cups rolled oats
2 cups all-purpose flour
1 teaspoon baking powder
½ teaspoon baking soda
1 teaspoon salt
1 cup chopped pecans

Melt margarine; beat in sugar. Add eggs, vanilla, and butter flavoring. Beat well until thoroughly mixed. Mix oats, flour, baking powder, baking soda, and salt. Add to egg mixture. Stir in pecans. Drop on ungreased cookie sheet in ½ teaspoon size. Bake in 350° oven for 12 minutes.
Yield: 60 cookies

Favorite Oatmeal Cookies

1 cup shortening
1 cup sugar
1 cup brown sugar
2 eggs
2 cups sifted all-purpose flour
1 teaspoon baking soda
½ teaspoon baking powder
½ teaspoon salt
2 cups quick-cooking oatmeal, uncooked
1 cup seedless raisins
½ cup chopped walnuts (or your choice)

Cream shortening and sugars. Add eggs and beat well. Sift together flour, baking soda, baking powder, and salt. Add to creamed mixture. Stir until flour is absorbed. Stir in oatmeal, raisins, and nuts. Drop dough from a teaspoon 2 inches apart on a greased cookie sheet. Bake at 350° for 10–12 minutes or until light brown. Allow to cool a minute before removing from cookie sheet.
Yield: 72 cookies

Bootsie's Heavenly Hash

5 (4-ounce) bars milk chocolate
1 (6.25-ounce) package miniature marshmallows
1 cup broken black walnuts

Melt chocolate over boiling water in a double boiler at high heat. Stir until smooth. Blend in marshmallows and nuts until coated with chocolate. Pour into greased 9-by-13-inch pan and refrigerate until firm, about 1 hour.
Yield: 36 servings

Cathedral Cookies

1 (12-ounce) package semisweet chocolate chips
4 tablespoons butter
2 eggs
½ teaspoon vanilla extract
¼ teaspoon salt
1 (10.25-ounce) package miniature colored marshmallows
1 cup chopped pecans
½ cup sifted confectioners' sugar

Melt chocolate chips in top of double boiler over 4 cups hot water. Add butter and mix well. Beat eggs well for 2 minutes and add to chocolate mixture. Add vanilla and salt. Cook at medium for 2 minutes. Take top pan off and let cool, about 1 hour. Add marshmallows and nuts. Cover wax paper with confectioners' sugar. Divide batter into thirds. Roll into long rolls 2 inches in diameter on wax paper. Chill overnight. Slice off when needed. The dough keeps indefinitely in refrigerator and freezes well.

Yield: 36 cookies

Chocolate Starlite Mint Surprises

3 cups all-purpose flour
1 teaspoon baking soda
½ teaspoon salt
8 tablespoons butter
½ cup shortening
½ cup brown sugar
1 cup granulated sugar
2 eggs
1 teaspoon vanilla extract
1 (1-pound) box solid mint chocolate candy wafers
24 pecan halves, if desired

Sift flour, baking soda, and salt together. Cream butter, shortening, brown sugar, and granulated sugar well. Blend in eggs, unbeaten. Beat well and add flour mixture gradually with 2 tablespoons water and 1 teaspoon vanilla. Refrigerate for at least 2 hours. Mold dough ½ teaspoon at a time around wafer. If desired, place pecan on top. Bake in 375° oven for 10–12 minutes.

Yield: 24 cookies

Note: The chocolate candy wafers are sometimes hard to find, but they are usually available on the candy aisle of chain grocery stores or online.

Nancy's Crunchy Date Bars

8 tablespoons butter
1 cup brown sugar
1 (8-ounce) package dates
½ cup coconut
1 teaspoon vanilla extract
½ cup broken pecans
2 cups crisped rice cereal
¼ cup confectioners' sugar

Cook butter and sugar over medium heat 10–15 minutes, stirring often. Cut dates in half and add to butter and sugar. Cook until dates are melted, about 10 minutes. Mash dates and let mixture cool. Add coconut, vanilla, nuts, and crisped rice cereal. After shaping in little cigar shapes, roll in confectioners' sugar. Refrigerate for 1 hour.

Yield: 36 bars

> Nancy was a dear friend of my mother.

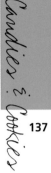
Melanie's Cookies

1 cup shortening
1 teaspoon salt
1 teaspoon grated lemon rind
1 teaspoon nutmeg
2 cups sugar
4 eggs
2 teaspoons baking powder
1 teaspoon baking soda
4 cups all-purpose flour
¼ cup milk
½ cup sugar

Beat together the shortening, salt, lemon rind, nutmeg, sugar, and eggs until smooth. Add baking powder and soda to flour and add milk. Add to egg mixture. Drop by teaspoon on greased cookie sheet. Flatten cookies with the bottom of a drinking glass covered with a damp cloth. Sprinkle with granulated sugar and bake in 300° oven for 15–18 minutes.

Yield: 60 cookies

Aloie's Frosted Nuts

8 tablespoons margarine
2 egg whites
1 cup brown sugar
4 cups pecan halves

Preheat oven to 275°. Melt margarine in 9-by-13-inch pan. Beat egg whites until stiff. Add brown sugar gradually. Stir in pecan halves, and spread over melted margarine in pan. Bake 45 minutes. Turn over every 10 minutes.

Yield: 4 cups

Aunt Polly's Divinity

2 cups sugar
½ cup light corn syrup
2 egg whites, stiffly beaten
1 teaspoon vanilla extract
1 cup chopped pecans

Cook sugar, ½ cup water, and corn syrup to soft ball stage (when mixture reaches 235° on your candy thermometer). Pour half of mixture into bowl with egg whites. Cook other half to hard ball stage (when mixture reaches 260° on your candy thermometer). Fold in egg white mixture and add vanilla. Beat until stiff, add nuts, and put on wax paper in ¾ teaspoon balls to cool. If desired, nut halves may be placed on top of candy instead of mixing chopped nuts in candy. If the candy does not harden, cook over water in a double boiler for 10–15 minutes longer.
Yield: 24 pieces

I have no idea who Aunt Polly is, but her divinity is delicious. Mom always made this at Christmas.

Peanut Butter Sticks

20 slices stale bread
½ cup peanut oil (or any cooking oil)
½ cup peanut butter

Trim crusts off stale bread, and cut into sticks. Use crust to make crumbs and set aside. Dry sticks of bread completely and toast lightly. Mix peanut oil and peanut butter together. Dip dry sticks into mix. Roll in fine crumbs made from crust. Let dry.
Yield: 24 sticks

Ellen's No-Flour Cookie

1 egg
1 cup brown sugar
1 cup crunchy peanut butter

Slightly beat egg and add brown sugar. Mix in peanut butter. Drop onto ungreased cookie sheet in ½ teaspoonfuls. Bake in 350° oven for 10–12 minutes.
Yield: 24 cookies

Ellen Hyams was the mayor of Bryson City in the 1970s.

Gammy's Creamy Pralines

1 cup firmly packed dark brown sugar
1 cup granulated sugar
$^2/_3$ cup undiluted evaporated milk
½ teaspoon vanilla extract
1 cup coarsely chopped pecans

Thoroughly combine brown sugar, granulated sugar, and milk. Stirring constantly, cook over medium heat until mixture forms soft ball (when mixture reaches 235° on your candy thermometer). Remove from heat, and add vanilla and nuts. Beat until thick. Drop onto wax paper in small amounts.

Yield: 18 pralines

Mother's (Dody's) Chocolate Fudge

3 cups sugar
$^1/_3$ cup unsweetened cocoa powder
¼ teaspoon salt
3 tablespoons light corn syrup
½ cup evaporated milk
3 tablespoons butter
1 teaspoon vanilla extract
½–1 cup chopped pecans or walnuts

Mix sugar, cocoa, salt, and syrup with milk and ½ cup water. Place in heavy saucepan over medium heat and bring to boil. Stir often to keep from sticking. Cook rapidly until mixture forms a soft ball when dropped into a cup of cold water or until it registers soft ball stage on a candy thermometer (235°). Start testing after cooking for 5 minutes. Remove from heat and add butter and vanilla. Let cool slightly and beat until spreading consistency. Add nuts and stir. Pour into a well-buttered dish. Cool and cut into squares.

Yield: 24 small pieces

My grandmother on my mother's side was Dody and on my father's side, Gammy. Both were amazing cooks (aren't all grandmothers?). You will find many of their recipes throughout this cookbook, but I believe that Gammy's Creamy Pralines and Dody's Chocolate Fudge are my favorites.

PIES &
PASTRIES

Our Heavenly Father, we come seeking Thee this morning, and we come praying for Thy continued mercy. We pray that we might somehow be like Thee and walk with Thee this day. We thank Thee for Thy strength and for this food. In Jesus' name we ask it. Amen.

Piecrust

1 egg
2 teaspoons white vinegar
5 cups all-purpose flour
½ teaspoon salt
2½ cups shortening

Break egg in cup. Add vinegar.
Fill cup with water to make 1 full cup.
Stir to break egg yolk. Combine flour
and salt in medium bowl. Cut in
shortening with pastry
blender. Add egg mixture to flour
mixture all at once and mix. Blend
until mixture holds together.
Divide into 6 balls. Put unused
portions in freezer.
**Yield: 6 (9-inch) crusts or
3 (9-by-13-inch) crusts**

Velda's Old-Fashioned Lemon Pie

4 tablespoons margarine, softened
2 cups sugar
4 eggs
juice and rind (grated) of 2 lemons
1 (9-inch) Piecrust (see above)

Cream margarine and sugar; add eggs,
one at a time, beating well after each
addition. Stir in lemon juice and rind;
mix well. Pour into unbaked Piecrust.
Bake at 350° for 40 minutes or until set
and lightly browned.
Yield: 1 (9-inch) pie or 8 servings

Coconut Caramel Pie

4 tablespoons butter
1 (7-ounce) package coconut
½ cup chopped pecans
1 (8-ounce) package cream cheese
1 (14-ounce) can sweetened
  condensed milk
1 (16-ounce) container whipped topping
2 (9-inch) deep-dish piecrusts, baked
1 (12-ounce) jar caramel ice cream topping

Melt butter in a large skillet.
Add coconut and pecans; cook until
golden brown, stirring frequently. Set
mixture aside. Combine cream cheese
and condensed milk; beat until
smooth. Fold in whipped topping.
Layer one-fourth cream cheese mixture
in each piecrust. Drizzle one-fourth
caramel topping over each. Sprinkle
one-fourth coconut mixture on each.
Repeat layers with remaining
ingredients. Cover and freeze
until firm, about 2 hours. Let pie
stand at room temperature 5 minutes
before slicing.
Yield: 2 (9-inch) pies or 16 servings

Quaker Pie

2/3 cup sugar
2 eggs, beaten
2/3 cup uncooked oatmeal
½ cup light corn syrup
2/3 cup melted margarine
¼ teaspoon salt
1 teaspoon vanilla extract
1 (9-inch) Piecrust (see opposite page)

Mix all ingredients together.
Pour into unbaked Piecrust.
Bake in 350° oven for 1 hour.
Yield: 1 (9-inch) pie or 8 servings

Velda's Swedish Pie

½ cup cake flour (or ½ cup minus
1 tablespoon all-purpose flour)
2 teaspoons baking powder
½ teaspoon salt
2 eggs
1 cup firmly packed light brown sugar
1 teaspoon vanilla extract
1 cup chopped pecans
1 cup peeled and cubed tart
Granny Smith apples
1 cup whipped topping

Combine flour, baking powder, and
salt; set aside. Beat eggs and sugar until
light and fluffy. Add flour mixture to
egg mixture, blending well. Stir in
vanilla, pecans, and apples. Spread
mixture in greased 10-inch pie plate.
Bake at 350° for 30 minutes. Cool, cut
into wedges, and serve with whipped
topping or other dairy topping.
Yield: 8 servings

Chocolate Chess Pie

1½ cups sugar
3 tablespoons unsweetened
   cocoa powder
2 eggs
4 tablespoons butter, melted
1 (6-ounce) can evaporated milk
1 teaspoon vanilla extract
1 (9-inch) Piecrust (see opposite page)

Mix all ingredients together and pour
into unbaked Piecrust. Bake for 1 hour
at 350°.
Yield: 1 (9-inch) pie or 8 servings

Helen's Chess Pie

3 eggs
1 cup sugar
½ cup brown sugar
1 tablespoon cornmeal
1 tablespoon all-purpose flour
8 tablespoons margarine, melted
1 teaspoon white vinegar
1 teaspoon vanilla extract
pinch of ground nutmeg, if desired
1 (9-inch) Piecrust (see page 142)

Preheat oven to 375°. Cream eggs and mix with sugars and cornmeal. Add flour and melted margarine. Stir in vinegar and vanilla, as well as nutmeg if desired. Pour into unbaked Piecrust and bake 10 minutes. Lower heat to 325° and bake 35 minutes.
Yield: 1 (9-inch) pie or 8 servings

Strawberry Pie

1 (9-inch) Piecrust (see page 142)
3 heaping tablespoons strawberry gelatin
3 heaping tablespoons cornstarch
1 cup sugar
2 cups strawberries
1 cup whipped topping

Bake Piecrust at 400° for 10–13 minutes. Set aside to cool. Cook gelatin, cornstarch, sugar, and 1 cup of very warm water on low heat until thick, about 10 minutes. Set aside. Slice strawberries and drain well. Put strawberries into Piecrust. Pour gelatin mixture over berries. Chill 1 hour. If desired, top with dab of whipped topping.
Yield: 1 (9-inch) pie or 8 servings

There's an old story told in the South about the origin of chess pie. At a church "dinner-on-the-ground" meeting, someone brought a delicious new pie that no one had tasted before. When asked what kind of pie it was, the baker answered, "Oh, it's jus' pie." Not understanding the Southern drawl too well, a visitor thought she said "chess pie." No, it isn't "a weed, floor planks, or skilled game" as was once listed under "chess" in Mr. Webster's dictionary! It's jus' pie! (It may not be a true story, but the story is told so often here in our mountains that it could easily be true!)

Dody's Banana Split Pie

3 medium bananas
1 tablespoon lemon juice
1 (9-inch) graham cracker crust
2 cups strawberry ice cream
1 cup whipped topping
1 (8-ounce) jar whole Maraschino cherries
2 tablespoons finely chopped pecans
½ cup Chocolate Quick Sauce

Slice bananas, lightly sprinkle with lemon juice, and arrange on bottom of piecrust. Stir ice cream to soften slightly, and spread over bananas. Freeze 1–2 hours. Spread whipped topping over ice cream. Top with cherries. Sprinkle with nuts. Freeze again. Let stand 30 minutes at room temperature before serving. Pour Chocolate Quick Sauce over each serving.
Yield: 1 (9-inch) pie or 8 servings

Chocolate Quick Sauce

1 (6-ounce) package chocolate chips
²/₃ cup evaporated milk
1 cup marshmallow cream

Cook chocolate chips and milk together over low heat until chocolate chips are melted. Beat in marshmallow cream until blended. Serve warm or cold.
Yield: 2 cups

Mrs. Garrett's Frozen Lemon Pie

²/₃ cup sugar
pinch of salt
3 eggs, separated
¼ cup lemon juice
1 tablespoon grated lemon rind
1 cup evaporated milk
1 (9-inch) Piecrust, baked (see page 142)
¼ cup graham cracker crumbs

Mix sugar, salt, egg yolks, lemon juice, and rind together. Cook in heavy boiler for 15 minutes; it will not thicken. Cool. Beat egg whites until stiff and fold into cooked mixture. Whip ice-cold evaporated milk until stiff and fold into the cooked mixture. Pour into baked Piecrust, cover with graham cracker crumbs, and freeze overnight.
Yield: 1 (9-inch) pie or 8 servings

Pineapple Cream Pie

1 (8-ounce) container cream cheese
1 can condensed milk
½ cup lemon juice
1 (20-ounce) can crushed pineapple
1 (16-ounce) container whipped topping
2 (9-inch) Piecrusts, baked (see page 142)

Cream together cream cheese and condensed milk; add lemon juice. Drain pineapple well. Add to whipped topping. Fold into cream cheese mixture. Pour into baked Piecrusts.
Yield: 2 (9-inch) pies or 16 servings

Velda's Grandmother's Pumpkin Pie

1½ cups canned pumpkin
¾ cup sugar
½ teaspoon salt
1 teaspoon ground cinnamon
½ teaspoon ground ginger
¼ teaspoon ground nutmeg
¼ teaspoon ground cloves
3 eggs, slightly beaten
1¼ cups milk
1 (6-ounce) can evaporated milk
1 (9-inch) Piecrust (see page 142)

Thoroughly combine pumpkin, sugar, salt, and spices. Blend in eggs, milk, and evaporated milk. Pour into unbaked Piecrust—this makes a large pie—and crimp edges high; the filling is generous. Bake at 400° for about 50 minutes. Cool on rack. If baking in glass pie pan, bake for 40 minutes at 400°.

Yield: 1 (9-inch) pie or 8 servings

Note: We always heat the two milks while we are making the pastry and add the other ingredients to the milk. Heating the milks gives the filling a little head start when the pie is put into the oven.

Nancy's Buttermilk Pie

4 tablespoons butter, melted
1 cup sugar
1 tablespoon all-purpose flour
2 eggs
½ cup buttermilk
½–¾ teaspoon vanilla extract
1 (9-inch) Piecrust (see page 142)

Mix well all ingredients except Piecrust, until smooth. Pour into Piecrust. Bake in 350° oven for 30–45 minutes.

Yield: 1 (9-inch) pie or 8 servings

Mrs. Mask's Pumpkin Pie

2 eggs
²/₃ cup sugar
1 ¾ cups canned pumpkin
1 teaspoon salt
1 tablespoon pumpkin pie spice
1½ cups milk
1 (9-inch) Piecrust (see page 142)

Beat eggs well. Add sugar and pumpkin. Sprinkle salt and pumpkin pie spice over mixture. Add milk. Stir all ingredients together well until smooth. Pour into unbaked Piecrust. Bake in 375° oven for 50–55 minutes or until sharp-bladed knife inserted near center comes out clean.

Yield: 1 (9-inch) pie or 8 servings

This recipe is also known as Pinto Bean Pie. One of my dear friends is Rita Mattox, and her husband, Johnny, does not like vegetables. He is strictly a meat and potatoes guy. One evening, my mom invited them to dinner and purposely served this pie for dessert to see if he would notice, and he did not. As he devoured it, we all convulsed in laughter. I am sure that was the last bean Johnny has eaten.

Mock Pecan Pie

1 (15-ounce) can pinto beans, cooked
4 eggs
1 (3.5-ounce) can flaked coconut
3 cups sugar
16 tablespoons margarine or butter, melted
1 cup chopped pecans
1 tablespoon vanilla extract
2 (9-inch) Piecrusts (see page 142)

Preheat oven to 300°. Drain and mash beans well, until smooth. In large mixing bowl, beat eggs until slightly thickened. Fold in remaining ingredients except Piecrust and mix well. Pour into Piecrusts. Bake for 40 minutes. Freezes well for later use.
Yield: 2 (9-inch) pies or 16 servings

E.J.'s Easy Pecan Pie

3 eggs
1 cup brown sugar
1 cup corn syrup (either light or dark)
pinch of salt
1 cup pecans (either whole or chopped)
½ teaspoon vanilla extract
1 (9-inch) Piecrust (see page 142)

Beat eggs until frothy. Add sugar, syrup, salt, pecans, and vanilla. Mix well. Pour into unbaked Piecrust and bake in 350° oven for 45 minutes–1 hour until set.
Yield: 1 (9-inch) pie or 8 servings

Mil's Peanut Butter Pie

2 cups milk
½ cup brown sugar
1 cup sugar
5 tablespoons cornstarch
½ cup evaporated milk
3 eggs, separated
⅛ teaspoon salt
¾ cup peanut butter
1 teaspoon vanilla extract
¼ teaspoon cream of tartar
2 (9-inch) Piecrusts, baked (see page 142)
2 cups whipped topping

Mix milk and sugars together and bring to boil in heavy boiler. Mix cornstarch, evaporated milk, and egg yolks together. Add to milk mixture and stir constantly until thick. Add salt and remove from stove. Beat in peanut butter and vanilla until blended. Beat egg whites with cream of tartar until stiff and fold in. Pour into baked Piecrusts. Cool and top with whipped topping.

Yield: 2 (9-inch) pies or 16 servings

Ryle's Blackberry Pie

6 cups blackberries, divided
1 (9-inch) Piecrust (see page 142)
1¼ cups sugar
3 tablespoons all-purpose flour
6 tablespoons butter
1 teaspoon lemon juice

Put half of berries in unbaked Piecrust. Mix sugar and flour together and put over top of berries. Add remaining berries and dot with butter. Sprinkle lemon juice over pie. Bake in 350° oven for 1 hour.

Yield: 1 (9-inch) pie or 8 servings

Note: You may omit bottom crust and cover the top instead. Slit the top crust or make a fancy design.

Jane's Fresh Peach Cobbler

2 cups sugar, divided
2 cups fresh sliced peaches
8 tablespoons butter
¼ teaspoon salt
1 teaspoon baking powder
¾ cup all-purpose flour
⅛ teaspoon ground cinnamon
¾ cup milk
¼ teaspoon almond extract

Mix 1 cup sugar with peaches and let stand while making batter. Melt butter in 2-quart casserole dish. Mix together 1 cup sugar, salt, baking powder, flour, and cinnamon. Beat in milk until no lumps. Add almond extract. Pour batter into the melted butter. Do not stir. Spoon peaches over top of batter. Do not stir. Bake in 350° oven for 45 minutes or until top is golden brown.

Yield: 6 servings

Hemlock Inn Fruit Cobbler

4 cups frozen sour (tart) cherries
2 cups sugar
3 tablespoons cornstarch
8 tablespoons butter or margarine
1 (9-by-13-inch) Piecrust (see page 142)

Put cherries in 9-by-13-inch pan. (Leave juice in cherries.) Mix sugar and cornstarch together and sprinkle over cherries. Dot with butter or margarine. Cover with Piecrust. Bake in 425° oven for approximately 30 minutes or until crust is golden brown.

Yield: 18 servings

Note: You may substitute peaches, blueberries, blackberries, or apples for cherries. With apples, add nutmeg and cinnamon to taste.

Easy Meringue

4 egg whites
¼ teaspoon cream of tartar
½ cup sugar

Beat egg whites (which should be at room temperature) and cream of tartar until foamy. Beat in sugar gradually. Beat until meringue forms stiff, glossy peaks. We use this meringue with chocolate, coconut cream, and lemon meringue pies.

Yield: Meringue for 1 pie

Creamy Lemon Meringue Pie

3 eggs, separated
1 (14-ounce) can sweetened condensed milk
½ cup lemon juice
1 teaspoon grated lemon rind
1 (9-inch) graham cracker piecrust
¼ teaspoon cream of tartar
⅓ cup sugar

Preheat oven to 350°. In medium bowl, beat egg yolks. Stir in milk, lemon juice, and rind. Pour into crust. In small bowl, beat egg whites with cream of tartar until foamy. Gradually add sugar, beating until stiff but not dry. Spread meringue on top of pie, sealing carefully to edge of crust. Bake 15 minutes or until meringue is golden brown. Cool. Chill 1 hour before serving. Refrigerate leftovers.

Yield: 1 (9-inch) pie or 8 servings

Hemlock Inn Chocolate Pie

2 egg yolks
1 cup sugar
1 cup milk
4 tablespoons margarine
2 heaping tablespoons all-purpose flour
2 heaping tablespoons unsweetened cocoa powder
1 teaspoon vanilla extract
1 (9-inch) Piecrust, baked (see page 142)
2 cups Easy Meringue (see at left)

Beat egg yolks slightly. Add sugar, milk, margarine, flour, and cocoa. Cook over medium heat, stirring constantly until thick, about 10 minutes. Add vanilla. Pour into baked Piecrust. Swirl on cooled Easy Meringue with spoon or spatula. Seal against crust edge to prevent shrinkage. Bake in preheated oven at 450° for 10–15 minutes or until meringue is brown-tipped.

Yield: 1 (9-inch) pie or 8 servings

Mil's Lemon Meringue Pie

2 cups sugar
5 heaping tablespoons cornstarch
3 egg yolks
$1/8$ teaspoon salt
2 tablespoons butter or margarine
juice of 3 lemons
rind of 2 lemons, grated
2 (9-inch) Piecrusts, baked (see page 142)
Easy Meringue (see opposite page)

Mix 2 cups water and sugar together and bring to boil. Mix well cornstarch, ½ cup water, 3 egg yolks, and salt, and add to sugar and water mixture. Stir constantly until mixture thickens. Add butter, lemon juice, and rind. Pour into baked Piecrusts. Swirl on cooled Easy Meringue with spoon or spatula and seal against crust edge. Bake in 375° oven for 10–12 minutes or until as brown as you like your pie to look.

Yield: 2 (9-inch) pies or 16 servings

Coconut Cream Pie

2 cups milk
2 cups sugar
5 heaping tablespoons cornstarch
3 egg yolks
½ cup evaporated milk
$1/3$ teaspoon salt
2 tablespoons butter or margarine
1 teaspoon vanilla extract
½ cup shredded coconut
2 (9-inch) Piecrusts, baked (see page 142)
Easy Meringue (see opposite page)

Mix together milk, sugar, and cornstarch and bring to boil. Meanwhile, beat egg yolks and add evaporated milk. Add to milk mixture. Stirring constantly, cook (still at soft boil) until thick. Add salt, butter, vanilla, and coconut. Stir until melted and blended. Total cooking time is about 15 minutes. Pour into baked Piecrusts and let cool completely. Swirl on cooled Easy Meringue with spoon or spatula and seal against crust edge. Bake in preheated oven at 450° for 10–15 minutes or until meringue is brown-tipped.

Yield: 2 (9-inch) pies or 16 servings

DESSERTS

Our Heavenly Father, we continue to be excited about Thy gospel, and our prayer is that this day we may learn to express it better. Our hearts are open wide that we might receive Thy grace and truly walk with Thee. We thank Thee for a new opportunity and for Thy strength, and especially for this food. In Jesus' name we ask it. Amen.

Judy's Blueberry Delight

1¼ cups graham cracker crumbs
1¼ cups sugar, divided
¼ cup softened butter
1 (8-ounce) container cream cheese
1 (9-ounce) container whipped topping
3 medium bananas
4 cups fresh blueberries

Combine graham cracker crumbs with ¼ cup sugar and softened butter, and blend well with fork. Press mixture firmly inside well-buttered 9-by-13-inch glass baking dish. Bake in 350° oven for 8 minutes. Let cool. Cream together cream cheese, 1 cup sugar, and whipped topping and mix thoroughly. Slice bananas and place on top of crust. Add alternately whipped topping mix and blueberries until dish is full. Let set for 2 hours in refrigerator.

Yield: 12 servings

Chocolate Fudge Sauce

8 ounces semisweet chocolate
2 cups sugar
1 tablespoon butter
1 (13-ounce) can evaporated milk
pinch of salt
1 teaspoon vanilla extract

Melt chocolate and sugar in a double boiler over hot water on high. Add butter, milk, and salt. Stir until smooth. Add vanilla. Use it as cake icing, or thin it with a small amount of warm water and drizzle over ice cream. It will keep in the refrigerator for 2 weeks.

Yield: 1½ cups, or enough for 20 sundaes

Chocolate Torte

8 tablespoons butter
1 cup self-rising flour
¾ cup chopped pecans
1 (8-ounce) container cream cheese
1 cup confectioners' sugar
1 (9-ounce) container whipped topping, divided
1 (6-ounce) package instant chocolate pudding
1 teaspoon almond extract

Melt butter in 9-by-13-inch baking dish. Sprinkle in flour and nuts, and spread with spoon until smooth. Bake in 350° oven for 15 minutes. Let cool. Cream the cream cheese and sugar. Mix together 1 cup whipped topping and cream cheese mixture. Spread over crust as first layer. Prepare instant chocolate pudding as directed and add almond flavoring. Spread over first layer. Top with remaining whipped topping. Refrigerate 2 hours before serving.

Yield: 12 servings

Note: Use lemon pudding instead of chocolate pudding to make Lemon Torte.

Annette's Glorified Brownies

8 tablespoons butter
1 cup sugar
2 eggs
1 teaspoon vanilla extract
2 (1-ounce) squares chocolate, melted
1 cup all-purpose flour
1 tablespoon baking powder
1 cup chopped pecans
12 marshmallows
1 cup Chocolate Icing

Cream butter and sugar. Add eggs that have been beaten well and vanilla. Add melted chocolate. Sift flour and baking powder together. Mix well and add to chocolate mixture. Add nuts. Pour into a greased 8-by-8-inch pan and bake at 350° for 30 minutes. When done, place marshmallows over top and return to oven until marshmallows are melted. Remove from oven and spread marshmallows. Cool. When cool, ice with Chocolate Icing.

Yield: 12 brownies

Chocolate Icing

1 tablespoon butter
1 cup confectioners' sugar
½ cup unsweetened cocoa powder
milk, if needed

Cream butter and add sugar with cocoa. If mixture gets too thick, add a small amount of milk.

Yield: 1 cup

Bootsie was my dad's cousin.

Annette was our next-door neighbor in Georgia.

Bootsie's Chocolate Dream Squares

20 graham crackers
16 tablespoons butter
3 (1-ounce) squares chocolate
3 eggs
2 cups confectioners' sugar
1 teaspoon vanilla extract
1½ cups chopped pecans
½ cup whipped topping

Roll out graham crackers to make crumbs. Melt butter and chocolate together and add to crumb mixture. Beat eggs and fold in sugar. Add vanilla and nuts to egg mixture. Put crumb mixture in greased 9-by-13-inch pan, and pour egg mixture on top. Refrigerate overnight. Serve with whipped topping.

Yield: 12 squares

Chocolate Lush

1 (15-ounce) angel food cake
1 (12-ounce) package chocolate chips
4 eggs, separated
½ cup milk
pinch of salt
2 tablespoons sugar
2 cups whipped topping
1 teaspoon vanilla extract

Break cake into pieces and put half of cake into buttered 9-by-13-inch pan. Melt chocolate chips in top of double boiler on high. Remove from stove and add egg yolks. Add milk slowly. Add pinch of salt. Add sugar gradually to stiff beaten egg whites. Fold into egg yolks, chocolate, and milk. Fold into whipped topping and vanilla. Pour half of mixture over cake. Add rest of cake and put remaining chocolate mixture on top. Chill overnight.
Yield: 12 servings

Chocolate Éclair Squares

7 ounces graham crackers
2 (3-ounce) packages instant French
   vanilla pudding
2 (8-ounce) containers whipped topping
1½ cups Chocolate Frosting

Layer half of graham crackers in 9-by-13-inch pan. Mix pudding as directed on package. Fold in half of whipped topping to pudding, and layer mixture on top of graham crackers. Add second layer of graham crackers and frost with remaining whipped topping. Pour Chocolate Frosting over top. Refrigerate for at least 1 hour before serving.
Yield: 18 éclairs

Chocolate Frosting

8 tablespoons butter
3 tablespoons unsweetened
   cocoa powder
2 cups confectioners' sugar
1 egg

Melt butter and cocoa on low heat until dissolved. Remove from heat. Add sugar. Beat until slightly cooled and add egg.
Yield: 1½ cups

Frozen Apricot Delight

6 eggs, separated
pinch of salt
1 cup sugar
1 cup puréed apricots
4 tablespoons apricot jam
4 tablespoons lemon juice
2 cups vanilla wafer crumbs
2 cups whipped topping

Beat egg yolks, salt, and sugar. Add puréed apricots, jam, and lemon juice. Cook slowly on low heat until mixture coats spoon. Cool. Spread half of crumbs into greased pan. Beat egg whites until stiff. Fold into whipped topping and then into custard. Pour into 9-by-13-inch pan. Top with remaining crumbs. Freeze until firm, about 1 hour.
Yield: 18 servings

Apple Goodie

8 cups peeled and chopped Granny Smith apples
¼ cup granulated sugar
2½ tablespoons cinnamon
2 cups brown sugar
2 cups oatmeal (uncooked)
2½ teaspoons baking soda
1¼ cups all-purpose flour
1¼ cups butter, melted

Place apples in buttered pie pan and cover with granulated sugar and cinnamon. Mix brown sugar, oatmeal, baking soda, flour, and butter. Sprinkle brown sugar mixture over apples. Bake in 325° oven for about 30 minutes or until apples are tender.
Yield: 10 servings

Irene's Lemon Freeze

1 (13-ounce) can evaporated milk
1 cup sugar
juice and rind of 3 lemons
1 (5.5-ounce) box vanilla wafers

Chill evaporated milk. Whip milk, adding sugar slowly. Add lemon juice and rind slowly. Crush vanilla wafers. Place half of the crumbs in the bottom of a 9-by-13-inch pan. Spread whipped milk over crumbs. Sprinkle remaining crumbs evenly over whipped milk. Freeze overnight until firm.
Yield: 8 servings

Easy Custard

Regular

8 cups whole milk
2 (3-ounce) packages instant
vanilla pudding
1 cup sugar
2 cups half-and-half
2 teaspoons vanilla extract

Sugar-Free

8 cups skim milk
2 (3-ounce) packages sugar-free instant
vanilla pudding
1 cup sucralose-based artificial sweetener
2 cups half-and-half
2 teaspoons vanilla extract

Mix all ingredients thoroughly with electric mixer on low for 1 minute. Refrigerate. Let stand 1–2 hours before serving.

Yield: 16 servings
Note: We use Splenda.

When Granddaddy Stevens was diagnosed as a brittle diabetic late in life, my grandmother Dody discovered this recipe. It's a real treat when you can't have sugar. I've given both the regular and sugar-free recipe.

Twig's Swedish Cream

2½ cups heavy whipping cream
1 cup sugar
1 tablespoon unflavored gelatin
2 cups sour cream
1 teaspoon vanilla extract
2 cups mixed fruit
¼ cup sugar

Put whipping cream, sugar, and gelatin into heavy boiler and heat over low heat, stirring constantly until gelatin is dissolved (about 45 minutes). Cool until it begins to thicken, about 1 hour. Add sour cream and vanilla. Refrigerate 2 hours. Serve with sugared fruit, such as strawberries, raspberries, or any kind of frozen mixed fruit.

Yield: 8 servings

Apple Dumplings

1 Pastry
12 cups peeled and quartered Granny Smith apples
4¼ cups sugar, divided
16 tablespoons butter
3½ teaspoons ground cinnamon, divided
¹/₃ cup apple cider vinegar
1½ teaspoons ground cloves

Roll pastry and cut into squares. Place apples in pastry squares and top with 1 teaspoon sugar and a dot of butter, and sprinkle evenly with ½ teaspoon cinnamon. Pinch edges together and seal. Put in greased 10-by-16-inch cobbler pan. Mix together 8 cups water, vinegar, remaining 4 cups of sugar, remaining 3 teaspoons of cinnamon, and cloves and boil gently for 5 minutes. Pour hot liquid around dumplings and bake in 375° oven for 45 minutes.
Yield: 12 servings

Pastry

4 cups all-purpose flour
2 cups shortening
1 heaping teaspoon salt
1 teaspoon white vinegar

Mix together flour, shortening, and salt until the mixture crumbles. Add 1⅛ cups ice water and vinegar, only enough to mix together well. Handle as little as possible. Make ahead of time and refrigerate overnight. Let come to room temperature before rolling. Leftover pastry can be frozen.
Yield: 1 Pastry

5-Minute Chocolate Mousse

1 teaspoon unflavored gelatin
½ cup sugar
¼ cup unsweetened cocoa powder
1 cup heavy cream (very cold)
1 teaspoon vanilla extract

Sprinkle gelatin over 1 tablespoon cold water in small bowl; stir and let stand 1 minute to soften. Add 2 tablespoons boiling water; stir until gelatin is completely dissolved (must be clear). Stir together sugar and cocoa in small, cold mixer bowl. Add cream and vanilla. Beat at medium speed until stiff peaks form, about 2 minutes. Pour in gelatin mixture and beat until well blended at low or medium speed. Spoon into serving dishes and chill about 30 minutes.
Yield: 4 (½-cup) servings

Mam-Maw's Boiled Custard

2 cups half-and-half
¼ cup sugar
pinch of salt
6 egg yolks
½ teaspoon vanilla extract

Mix half-and-half, sugar, and salt together in heavy boiler. Scald (do not boil). Pour mixture into slightly beaten egg yolks and stir thoroughly. Pour back into boiler and cook over medium heat for 5 minutes (no longer than 7 minutes) or until mixture coats spoon. Stir constantly. Cool (about 45 minutes). Add vanilla. Stir well. Strain. Pour into pitcher and put in refrigerator 1 hour.

Yield: 4 servings

This was my great-grandmother's recipe. In trying to make it through the years, it never looked exactly like hers. One day it dawned on me that she always saved the cream for her boiled custard. For those of you too young to know what that means, let me explain that before we bought homogenized milk, we bought whole milk. The cream rose to the top of the container, and if you needed whipping cream, you just skimmed the cream off the top. If not, you just shook the milk bottle and had regular milk. When I realized that this is what Mam-Maw had done, I tried half-and-half and it worked!

For special occasions such as family reunions or church suppers, she always poured the custard in a punch bowl. She whipped another half cup of cream and placed dabs on top of custard. This was called floating islands!

Banana Pudding

1 (5.5-ounce) box vanilla wafers
4 medium bananas
1 cup crushed pineapple (reserve juice)
½ cup coarsely chopped pecans
1 egg
½ cup sugar
2 tablespoons all-purpose flour
1 cup whipped topping

Place half of wafers in 8-by-8-inch pan. Thinly slice bananas lengthwise and place on wafers. Put pineapple over bananas. Sprinkle with nuts. Repeat all layers a second time. Combine egg, sugar, reserved pineapple juice, and flour and cook over low heat, stirring constantly until smooth. Pour over banana mixture. Chill several hours. Top with whipped topping.

Yield: 8 servings

Inez's Miniature Cheesecakes

¾ cup sugar
2 (8-ounce) blocks cream cheese
3 eggs, separated
3 cups graham cracker crumbs, divided
¾ cup sour cream
2 tablespoons sugar
½ teaspoon vanilla extract

Mix ¾ cup sugar, cream cheese, and beaten egg yolks until light and fluffy. Fold in beaten egg whites. Butter miniature muffin tins generously. Take 1 teaspoon graham cracker crumbs per well and sift in tins. Cover tins with wax paper and shake to completely coat the tins. Fill tins ¾ full with cream cheese mixture, and bake 15–20 minutes at 350°. Remove cakes from tin while warm. They will have an indentation. Mix together sour cream, 2 tablespoons sugar, and vanilla in small baking dish and bake at 400° for 5 minutes. Put half teaspoon on each cake in center. Freeze 1–2 hours.

Yield: 48 miniature cakes

Estelle's Fruitcake Squares

1 cup brown sugar
8 tablespoons butter
2 eggs
1 cup all-purpose flour
1 teaspoon vanilla extract
1 cup pecan halves
1½ cups candied cherries
6 slices candied pineapple

Cream brown sugar with butter.
Add eggs, flour, and vanilla. Grease
9-by-13-inch pan and lightly flour.
Spread pecans over bottom of pan.
Spread batter over nuts. Chop cherries
and pineapple, and press fruit into
batter. Mash fruit into top very well.
Bake in 350° oven for 30–40 minutes.
Cool before cutting.
Yield: 24 squares

Mom always
fixed these for
the holidays.
Estelle was
one of my Girl
Scout leaders.

One winter afternoon,
Myrtle Mask, our cook,
called up to the inn to
announce that she had
a surprise. Mrs. Mask
lived on the property,
not too far away, and was
always experimenting
with new recipes.
We waited anxiously and
were not disappointed
when she arrived with
this delicious dessert.
Thus, the recipe was
named Myrtle's Surprise.
You will find many
recipes by Myrtle
in this cookbook.

Myrtle's Surprise

1 (3-ounce) package orange gelatin
1 (3-ounce) package pineapple gelatin
1 cup sugar
1¾ cups crushed pineapple
juice of 1 lemon
2 cups whipped topping, divided
1 (15-ounce) angel food cake

Combine the two gelatins and soften
with 4 teaspoons cold water. Add sugar
and 1 cup boiling water. Stir. Add
pineapple and lemon juice. Mix well.
Put in refrigerator until almost
thickened, about 30 minutes. Fold
1 cup whipped topping into gelatin
mixture. Line 9-by-13-inch glass
baking dish with wax paper. Crumble
half of cake in pan. Spread all gelatin
mixture on this. Crumble half of cake
on top of mixture. Put in refrigerator to
set overnight. Ice cake with remaining
1 cup whipped topping.
Yield: 18 servings

Myrtle's Cherry Yum-Yum

2½ cups graham cracker crumbs
1½ cups sugar, divided
12 tablespoons margarine, melted
1 (8-ounce) container cream cheese
2 cups whipped topping
~~**1 cup milk**~~
2 (21-ounce) cans cherry pie filling

Combine cracker crumbs, ½ cup sugar, and margarine. Mix well. Blend cream cheese, 1 cup sugar, whipped topping, ~~and cold milk~~. Spread half of crumb mixture in 9-by-13-inch baking dish. Add half of cream cheese mixture. Spread on cherry pie filling. Add remaining cream cheese mixture. Top with remaining crumbs. Refrigerate several hours.

Yield: 18 servings

Note: This is also good with blueberry pie filling.

Pumpkin Ice Cream

8 cups vanilla ice cream, softened
2 cups canned pumpkin
1 cup sugar
1 teaspoon ground cinnamon
1 teaspoon ground nutmeg
1 teaspoon ground ginger
½ teaspoon salt
1 cup chopped pecans
1 (16-ounce) bag gingersnaps
1 (8-ounce) container whipped topping
1 cup pecans, toasted

Blend softened ice cream with pumpkin, and add sugar, spices, salt, and pecans. Line oblong 14-by-8-inch pan with whole gingersnaps and cover with half of ice cream mixture. Allow to set in freezer for 1 hour. Add another layer of gingersnaps and remainder of ice cream mixture. Cover and freeze overnight. Cut in squares to serve, and top with whipped topping and one whole toasted pecan.

Yield: 18 servings

Carole's Pumpkin Torte

½ cup chopped dates
½ cup chopped pecans
$^1/_3$ cup plus 2 tablespoons all-purpose flour, divided
4 tablespoons margarine
1 cup brown sugar
$^2/_3$ cup canned pumpkin
1 teaspoon ground cinnamon
½ teaspoon ground nutmeg
¼ teaspoon baking soda
½ teaspoon ground ginger
1 teaspoon orange flavoring
½ teaspoon baking powder
2 eggs
½ cup whipped topping, if desired

Mix dates, pecans, and 2 tablespoons flour together and set aside. Mix all other ingredients together (except whipped topping) and add to date mixture. Bake in ungreased 9-by-13-inch dish 25 minutes in 350° oven. Cut in squares. Top with whipped topping if desired.
Yield: 10 servings
Note: This dessert can be frozen after it's baked.

Mort's Banana Pudding

3 (3-ounce) packages instant banana pudding
4 cups milk
1 cup sour cream
1 (8-ounce) container whipped topping
1 (11-ounce) box vanilla wafers

Mix pudding and milk as noted on pudding box. Add sour cream and whipped topping. Layer with vanilla wafers.
Yield: 24 servings *↓ Bananas*

I am sure that in the early years, my husband, Mort, often felt overwhelmed in the family business. Just two years after we moved to the inn, my mom was diagnosed with cancer, and then two years after that, I was diagnosed with multiple sclerosis. Mort's role expanded quickly. He became the innkeeper, the host, the clerk, and the handyman, in addition to being the husband, the dad, and the son-in-law. As the years go on, nothing seems to slow down Mort, and banana pudding helps him through it all. This is his favorite.

Our Father, for these friends
who sustain us socially, for this
food that sustains us physically,
and for Thy saving grace that
does sustain us spiritually, we
give Thee thanks. Amen.

Lord,
Our plates are full;
Our friends are near;
Our hearts are warm;
Our thanks sincere.
Amen.

Our Heavenly Father, how glad
we are to come to Thee as this
day closes, and we come with
thanksgiving in our hearts.
We thank You for this lovely
day and for Thy mercy and
continued watchcare.
We thank you for good
friends and answered prayers,
and especially now for this food.
In Jesus' name we ask it.
Amen.

Weights and Measures

Abbreviations:

cm.........centimeter
g...........gram
kg.........kilogram
ml.........milliliter
oz......... ounce
lb..........pound

English:

1 tablespoon.....3 teaspoons
¼ cup............... 4 tablespoons or
2 fluid ounces
⅓ cup............... 5 ⅓ tablespoons
½ cup............... 8 tablespoons or
4 fluid ounces
1 cup................ 16 tablespoon or
8 fluid ounces
2 cups...............1 pint or
16 fluid ounces
4 cups...............1 quart or
32 fluid ounces
4 quarts............1 gallon
8 quarts............1 peck
4 pecks............1 bushel
1 pound............16 ounces

Metric:

Liquid or Dry Measures:
¼ cup.......59 ml
⅓ cup.......79 ml
½ cup.......118 ml
⅔ cup.......152 ml
¾ cup.......176 ml
1 cup........237 ml
2 cups...... 473 ml
4 cups...... 946 ml

Dry Measures:

1 tablespoon........ 14.9 ml
1 teaspoon............. 4.9 ml
½ teaspoon........ 2.5 ml
¼ teaspoon......... 1.2 ml

Volume Measures:

1 gallon................ 3.79 liters
1 quart................. 0.95 liters
1 pint................... 0.48 liters

The actual weight of 1 oz. = 28.35 g

Weights	Grams
½ oz....................	14 g
1 oz......................	28 g
2 oz......................	57 g
3 oz......................	85 g
4 oz......................	113 g
5 oz......................	142 g
6 oz......................	170 g
8 oz......................	227 g
10 oz....................	284 g
12 oz....................	340 g
1 lb......................	454 g
2½ lb....................	0.91 kg
3 lb......................	1.35 kg

Table of Equivalents

Food Equivalents

apples...................................3 pounds = about 2 quarts, sliced
baking powder.....................1 t. single-acting = ¾ t. double-acting
cheese..................................1 pound = 4½ cups
cottage cheese......................1 pound = 2 cups
chocolate, unsweetened........1 square (1 oz.) = 3–4 T. grated chocolate
cornstarch...........................1 T. = 2 T. flour
crackers, graham..................3 cups crumbs = 30–36 crackers
crackers, salted....................1 cup fine crumbs = 20 crackers
dates, pitted........................1 pound = 2 cups
eggs......................................whole..............1 egg = about 3 T.
                                                              1 cup = 5–6 eggs
                                          whites ....1 white = about 2 T.
                                                              1 cup = 8–10 whites
                                          yolks ....1 yolk = about 1 T.
                                                              1 cup = 14–16 yolks
figs, chopped........................1 pound = 3 cups
flour.....................................unsifted................................1 pound = 3 cups
                                          all-purpose, sifted once.....................1 pound = 3¾ cups
                                          cake, sifted once................................1 pound = 2 cups
gelatin, unflavored...............1 envelope = 1 T.
lemon...................................1 average size = 2–3 T. juice, 3 T. rind
lentils...................................1 cup dry = 2 cups cooked
macaroni...............................1–1¾ cups dry (4 oz.) = 2¼ cups cooked
marshmallows.......................½ pound = 30 standard size
                                          1 standard size = 10 miniature
noodles.................................1½–2 cups dry (4 oz.) = 2¼ cups cooked
prunes, dried........................1 pound, dried = 2½ cups
                                          1 pound, cooked = 4 cups
punch....................................1 gallon = serves approx. 20
                                          12 quarts = 96 punch glasses
raisins...................................1 pound, seeded = 2½ cups
                                          1 pound, seedless = 3 cups
rice.......................................1 cup, raw = 3–3½ cups cooked
                                          1 cup, precooked = 2 cups
shortening, butter.................1 pound = 2 cups
                                          ½ pound = 2 sticks
                                          1 stick = ½ cup or 8 T.
spaghetti...............................1–1¼ cup raw (4 oz.) = 2½ cups cooked
sugar ....brown, sieved and packed.................1 pound = 2⅛ cups
                                          confectioners', sifted..........................1 pound = about 4 cups
                                          granulated...1 pound = 2⅛ cups
yeast.....................................1 cake yeast = 1 level T. active dry
                                          1 pkg. dry yeast = 1 level T. active dry
vanilla wafers.......................1 cup crumbs = about 22 wafers
zwieback...............................1 cup crumbs = 8–9 slices

Index

Left to right: Andrew, Jeanette, Mort, Lainey, John Thomas, Sarah, and Steven

Website:	HemlockInn.com
Phone:	(828) 488-2885
E-mail:	hemlock@dnet.net
Address:	*Recipes from Our Front Porch* c/o Hemlock Inn P.O. Box 2350 Bryson City, NC 28713